AMSTERDAM IN THE AGE OF REMBRANDT

Amsterdam
IN THE AGE
OF REMBRANDT

By John J. Murray

DAVID & CHARLES
NEWTON ABBOT

BY JOHN J. MURRAY

Student Guidebook to English History
Essays in Modern European History Honouring W. T. Morgan
An Honest Diplomat at the Hague
Sjomakternas Expedition till Östersjön I 1715
The Heritage of the Middle West (editor)
Amsterdam in the Age of Rembrandt

ISBN 0 7153 5528 7

© the University of Oklahoma Press,
Publishing Division of the University 1967

First published in Great Britain 1972

Reproduced and Printed in Great Britain by
Redwood Press Limited Trowbridge & London
for David & Charles (Publishers) Limited
Newton Abbot Devon

To Jack WHO MET AMSTERDAM WITH ME

Preface

THIS BOOK in part is a result of my many years of study on the influence of the Low Countries on sixteenth- and seventeenth-century Britain. Throughout much of the latter century. Amsterdam was the city that most shaped English life and thought just as Antwerp had been a hundred years earlier. The two cities at their heights were the queen cities of Europe from which the best and sometimes the worst of the Renaissance was spread throughout much of Northern Europe. Amsterdam during the life spans of the artist Rembrandt and the poet Vondel was perhaps the most cosmopolitan city in the world, trafficking in both goods and ideas.

Many groups and individuals have assisted me through the years. The Folger Shakespeare Library in Washington and the Newberry Library in Chicago each have given more than one research fellowship, and the Social Science Research Council, with a faculty research fellowship, made a year's study in Europe possible. Louis B. Wright of the Folger Library has always been willing to give encouragement and advice at times when they were most desperately needed. The staffs of the British Museum, the Cambridge University Library, the Royal Library at The Hague, and Coe College have been most patient and helpful. I am especially indebted so far as this book is concerned to Simon Hart of the Amsterdam City Archives. He put his vast knowledge of the city and his time at my disposal, and for that and his friendliness I am most grateful.

Professor M. de la Fontaine-Verwey opened his seventeenth-century house on the Prinsengracht to me and Mr. A. Perfors, the administrator of the Royal Palace, allowed me to go through that magnificent baroque structure at an inconvenient time to him and his staff. The city architect, S. I. S. Wichers, patiently explained urban growth and architecture as it was in the seventeenth century. To them I am deeply indebted as I am to Mrs. Ewight, that transplanted Amsterdamer on the Newberry staff.

I also appreciate the fact that President Joseph McCabe and the Board of Trustees of Coe College have been most generous with leaves and light teaching loads which have given me time to study and write. Most of all I should like to express my gratitude to Blair Stewart and William Towner, directors of The Newberry Library Seminar in the Humanities of the Associated Colleges of the Midwest. Most of the writing of this book was done while I was a faculty fellow with the Seminar. My co-faculty fellow, Richard van Fossen of the Cornell College English Department, read the manuscript and offered many helpful comments. I am also grateful to the University of Oklahoma Press for inviting me to contribute to the Centers of Civilization Series.

Preface

I would be remiss not to mention my wife, Betty, and my two sons Jack and Mike. Continued absences from the home front forced the first often to play the role of both father and mother and the last two to do chores which they could have avoided had I been there. They indeed made sacrifices so that I could woo Amsterdam.

The books and authors who have added to my understanding of Amsterdam and the Low Countries are legion. Some I have mentioned in the text; others I can in a work of this sort thank only collectively. The selected reading list contains a few standard works by Dutch authors and a few titles in English should readers desire to pursue the story of Amsterdam further. The books on the subject are buttressed by Dutch paintings hanging in museums throughout the world. A recent two-volume edition of Rembrandt's drawings with notes by Professor Seymour Slive, a fellow Fulbright scholar of some years back, depicts the Amsterdam of the artist in a language beyond linguistics. Today as then it is a "surprising" city, a joy to know and study.

JOHN J. MURRAY

CEDAR RAPIDS, IOWA
AUGUST 26, 1966

Contents

	Preface	*page* ix
1.	The City	3
2.	The House the *Heeren* Built	20
3.	Market of the World	48
4.	The Dissemination of Knowledge	91
5.	Parnassus on the IJ	117
	Selected Readings	176
	Index	178

MAP

Amsterdam: the "plan of the three canals"   *page* 2

xiii

AMSTERDAM IN THE AGE OF REMBRANDT

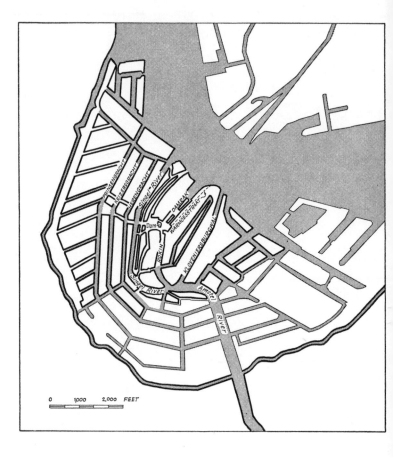

Amsterdam: the "plan of the three canals"

*Developed 1612–65 and sufficient for the town's expansion until the
middle of the nineteenth century. Heavy black lines indicate the
built-up area in the age of Rembrandt.*

CHAPTER ONE

The City

AMSTERDAM, a city rich in history, outstanding in art, and colorful in appearance, is closely linked with the sea, as indeed is the entire history of the Low Countries. The Dutch say, "He who cannot master the sea is not worthy of the land," and, "God made the world, but the Dutch made Holland." The same can be said even more appropriately for Amsterdam and the Amsterdamers, for they reversed the process of evolution. In the world there was first the sea and the mire with life and man emerging from the mucky chaos. There was also sea and mire where the Amstel sluggishly emptied into the Zuider Zee—now the IJsselmeer. River and sea joined in a large protective inlet called the IJ or Y. To that place man came. Instead of rising from the mud he built on it a city of poise, of courage, of real beauty, which since the beginning of the seventeenth century has been one of the most unusual cultural centers of the world.

His was a never-ending battle against the forces of nature with both the sea and the wet hinterlands challenging the city's growth and expansion. Fate and Dutch

3

doggedness set Amsterdam on a mud flat, but forty feet below the surface was a sturdy sand bank. Subsequently Amsterdam became a city resting on piles. These ranged in length from thirteen to fifty-nine feet. They were driven into the sand, and houses, shops, wharves, and public buildings were constructed on them. The City Hall, now the Royal Palace, considered to be the greatest achievement of Dutch Renaissance architecture, rested on 13,659 such supports averaging about forty feet in length. Recently one was pulled and found to be probably in as good condition as the day it was driven. Small wonder that admiring visitors commented that Amsterdam was a city of inverted forests where the trees grew down instead of up.

The land itself was fertile, and when drained could be converted into market squares and gardens. Canals became avenues of commerce and picturesque bridges spanned the islands which comprised the city. Modern Amsterdam far outstrips Venice in its number of canals, which form ninety islands joined by over four hundred bridges. In the seventeenth century there was even more open water and inland quays, much of which is now covered by paved roads and buildings.

Not all travelers found so much water to their liking. The Englishman, Owen Feltham, considered Holland the "great Bog of Europe . . . an universal Quag-mire." It was a "green Cheese in pickle," devoid of trees and stones, where gold was more plentiful than stones and where the spiders were as large as shrimp. In Amsterdam a startled horse could expose a person "to two deaths at once, breaking your neck or drowning." It was a great place for despairing lovers, for every corner afforded them "willow to make a Garland on," and most of the dwellings stood "like privies in mooted-houses, hanging still over the water."

Ironically most of the water was the wrong kind. The city was continually faced with shortages of "sweet" drinking water. James Howell, author of *Epistolae Hoelianae*, visited Amsterdam in 1619 and noticed that the city had neither well, fountain, nor fresh spring water and that it was dependent on cisterns or fresh water brought in by boat. Neither of these expediencies could produce sufficient uncontaminated water. Consequently disease abounded. The situation was aggravated by people throwing all sorts of filth into the canals, "which causes ill Scents and Fumes which is a nasty thing." Saskia and Titus, the wife and son of Amsterdam's most renowned artist, Rembrandt van Rijn (1609–69), were just two out of thousands who died from respiratory disorders. To cope with the situation a group of Frenchmen fortified themselves with "a good Dose of old Hock every Day . . . as the better sort of Dutch do and the common with a Cup of *Nantz*." The well-known Dutch addiction to drink during this period might merely have been preventive medicine.

Although Amsterdam owed its very existence to the sea, its location was not conducive to the making of a great maritime port. Amsterdam's and Holland's greatest poet, Joost van der Vondel (1587–1679), who knew his Amsterdam history well, described the shallow damp area along the IJ and Amstel where the first inhabitants settled.

Where now the columns of the city stand
In earlier times were hovels made with reeds.

Wet fisher-folk quick Amstel fish did catch
By filling bow-nets with the fishes' feed.
Now merchants under arch and roof
Inside the Beurs are wholly weatherproof.

Up to the sixteenth century the city was able to maintain its position as the country's leading commercial and trading center by keeping its vessels small enough to navigate in shallow waters through a fairly deep channel leading into the city. As the size of the ships increased, the *Pampus* mudbank blocking the entrance to the harbor became a real menace and it became impossible to keep the channel clear by dredging. In 1690, Meeuwes Bakker invented the "ships camels," huge drums filled with water and chained under the ships. When pumped dry, they elevated the ships so they could slide across the bank. This make-shift system lasted for 135 years. Thus it was only by sheer ingenuity and effort that Amsterdam during the age of Rembrandt and Vondel was able to bring the riches of East and West to its warehouses along the quays.

The IJ is on the western side of the Zuider Zee. The series of concentric circles from a stone dropped in it would go up the Singel and the Amstel in a southwesterly direction. Through such an imaginary series of half circles meandered the Amstel approaching the city from a south southeasterly direction and reaching the city walls about where the Stadthouders Kade now is. Slightly to the southwest was the city gate on the road to Utrecht. Just beyond the Herengracht the river took a sharp westerly turn, and at the Muntplein it divided with the Singel which carried part of the water around what were once the medieval city walls. The main stream, however, continued north to the Dam, the square which was the heart of the city. This stretch was called the Rokin. That part of the river joining the Dam with the sea was the Damrak, a large open body of water with streets on both sides, and countless ships moored to the docks. When it reached the IJ, it flowed out into the Zuider Zee through a series of dikes and sluices.

Dutch cartography makes it easy to trace Amsterdam's growth in the seventeenth century. A 1597 map done by Pieter Bast shows that the city was already tending towards its usual crescent shape. The city had extended westward to the Herengracht and on the eastern side the wharves and industries connected with shipping had been surrounded by new fortifications. Town boundaries in the middle of the sixteenth century had been the Singel on the west and the Kloveniersburgwal and the Oude Wal on the east.

During the lives of Rembrandt and Vondel the exquisite Weigh House stood in the middle of the Dam. Built between 1563 and 1566, it was the hub of the commodity market, and around it innumerable street peddlers hawked their wares. Here the sober garb of the burgher aristocracy and the clergy contrasted sharply with the colorful costumes of the lower classes and the finery of plumed gallants both native and foreign. Horses, animals for slaughter, all sorts of carts, beer kegs, and wine casks continually moved across the square, and the hustle and bustle of the moment has been captured and preserved on the canvases of Cornelis de Bie (1621–44) and Jacob Ruysdael (1626–82).

By the seventeenth century the butchers no longer had their guildhall on the main square, but the fishmongers remained very much in evidence. Although the fresh-water-fish market was on the Rokin, ocean fish were sold in open stalls on the Dam, which was the largest market of its kind in the world. It provided food for the citizens and capital for investment. It was also a favorite spot for tourists who marveled at the versatility in profanity displayed by the fishwives as they coarsely entreated customers to buy or insulted those who refused, regardless of rank and in a manner that made the ladies of Billingsgate seem like Sunday school teachers. Also around the Dam were shops specializing in southern fruits, spices, and drugs. Early every December, in spite of Calvinist divines, the St. Nicholas market was held when the city's favorite saint traveled from the Dam to the Oude Kerk through lanes of singing children while hucksters did a land-office business in cookies and candies.

Both the Dam and the Damrak had many restaurants and grog shops. Many of these were located in cellars often at the mercy of high tides. Yet space was at such a premium that the cellars often rented at between 400 and 500 guilders per year. The pubs pushed beer and gin while the coffee houses featured a coffee-milk drink spiced with nutmeg and licorice. Dutch cuisine seems not to have been universally acclaimed. One visitor commented: "The Dutch are ill Cooks, and verifie the proverb that God sends Meat, and the Devil the Dresser." The three most important buildings on the Dam in addition to the Weigh House were the Nieuwe Kerk, the City Hall, and the Exchange. They symbolized the religious, political, and economic life of the city.

In Rembrandt's time, the Warmoesstraat was the economic heart of Amsterdam, and it was there that the solid base of the city's trade supremacy was laid. By 1625 not many of the leading merchants lived there. They had moved out to the Fluweelenburgwal or the Herengracht. Others would follow as they sought areas in the city where homes were built more for gracious living than for the storage of commodities or the making and bartering of goods.

The Warmoesstraat is in the oldest part of the city and dates back to its beginnings. Here was the St. Olofskapel, the Oude Kerk, St. Anthonie's Weigh House and Market Place. The street paralleled the Damrak, and went from the back of the fish market on the Dam to St. Olaf's gate. Beyond the gate was the St. Nicholas Kerk, while running off the Warmoesstraat towards the Oude Kerk were numerous small alleyways filled with taverns and brothels frequented by sailors of many nations and the men and women who lived off them.

The Warmoesstraat was a hub of activity and a riot of color. At Number 39 and later at Number 110, Vondel composed and carried on the family business. The market place handled many commodities and it was only a short trip across a bridge to the Dam. Tradesmen's shops were easily identified by highly decorated swinging signboards and by elaborately carved stones set into the façades (*gevels*) of the buildings. These could illustrate the trade or the family. Just as the sign of the unicorn indicated an apothecary shop, the two clasped hands on the *gevel* stone on the Vondel stocking shop signified that the family could be trusted. Above the signboards were the famous gabled roofs of Amsterdam, the most common on the Warmoesstraat being the stepped gable and a plain one shaped like a triangle (*tuitgevel*).

Under the signboards and behind the façade stones, business flourished. The Warmoesstraat was to trading and selling what the Dam was to finance and exchange. Drapers displayed costly French silks and Oriental cottons, and their warehouses were stocked with more moderately priced Dutch cloths such as those the English called the "new draperies," or corduroys perhaps made by the Pilgrim Fathers working in Leiden. Presiding over the trade were the Syndics who still look down from Rembrandt's painting or peer forth from a box of Dutch Master cigars. Shoppers visited the showrooms of jewelers and goldsmiths, whose arts were to be enriched by Jewish refugees. Hatters, shoemakers, hosiers, tradesmen great and small along with the street vendors were "purveyors to the wealth and vanity of an opulent population." Warmoesstraat houses were homes, stores, warehouses, and workshops combined.

The city grew. By 1612 Amsterdam's population was fifty thousand inhabitants. This number doubled in ten years and doubled once again in the next forty. By mid-century Amsterdam had two hundred thousand residents plus the foreign seamen, tradesmen, politicians, refugees, and visitors who constantly flowed through the city gates. It was the most cosmopolitan city in Europe. The different racial and ethnic groupings became assimilated in the broad stream of Netherlandish culture, and gave a special twist to Amsterdam life. James Howell wrote his father in 1619: "I am lodg'd in a Frenchman's house who is one of the Deacons of our *English Brownists* Church here; it is not far from the synagogue of the *Jews*, who have a free and open exercise of their Religion here."

The synagogue mentioned was not the magnificent one

built by the Sephardim in the 1670's and which still
stands today. By 1700 most foreign congregations had their
own places of worship. German Jews of the Ashkenazem
went to their great synagogue on the Hoogstraat, and their
Lutheran countrymen along with the Scandinavians attended the famous round church on the east side of the
Singel. German Calvinists for the most part joined Dutch
congregations. English Anabaptists were in and out of
Mennonite congregations, sometimes meeting in "a great
house," while their Calvinist countrymen gathered in the
historic English Church in the Begijnhof just off Kalverstraat. English Barrowists and Quakers were much in evidence and French Huguenots could be found on a Sunday
morning at their church which still stands on the Walenpleintje (Walloon Square). Greek Orthodox services were
held for Armenians and other Levantines in the Dijkstraat, and foreign Catholics might join Dutch coreligion-
ists in the Church of *Onze Liever Heer op Zolder* (Our
Beloved Lord in the Attic) located on the Oude Zijds
Voorburgwal and now the Catholic museum.

The largest number of "strangers" came from the South
Netherlands, but the Jewish community, whose members
still peer forth in pain and sorrow, in joy and security,
from the immortal works of Rembrandt, were the most
colorful. The Sunday market of the Jewish quarter no
longer exists. No more can one go there to browse for
books or haggle over the prices of pickles, kosher foods,
furs, glassware, and "the sumptuous but sordid costume
jewelry with which Rembrandt decked out his rabbis,
Biblical princes, and Jewish brides." Yet their synagogue
is a proof of their opulence. Among the priceless treasures
collected there is a copy of the "Holy Story" done by

Manasseh ben Israël and illustrated by neighbor Rembrandt van Rijn who lived at 2 Jodenbreestraat (the second house on Wide-of-the-Jews Street).

The new inhabitants contributed much to the city, but they overloaded Amsterdam's housing capabilities. To meet the challenge a Board of Directors for City Works was formed in 1595 with Frans Oetgens head of the building program. Serving with him were Hendrik Staets, master of the city carpenters, Cornelis Danckertsz., the city master mason, and Hendrik de Keyser (1565–1621), the city master sculptor and carver. These men were to play significant roles in the great expansion of Amsterdam. In 1612, De Keyser was selected to be the city's first public architect.

Two years before his appointment the famous "plan of the three canals" had been adopted by the city fathers. Carried out between 1612 and 1655 and best illustrated by a map drawn by J. de Ram (c. 1681), the plan was a masterpiece in land reclamation. Through the use of piles and cowhides to provide stable foundations, the project extended the boundaries of the walled area of the town from 180 to 720 hectares.

The territory to be cleared and drained was acquired by the city, divided into lots, and resold with strict building regulations. On the west side of the city a spacious place was reserved for small business and industry and for lower middle-class housing. The upper classes were to be located on three grand *grachts* (canals): the Herengracht, the Keizersgracht, and the Prinsengracht in that order of preference, social prestige, and cost. Every third island on the IJ running from east to west was filled in, and a new city wall consisting of twenty-six bulwarks was constructed in a long curve. Windmills were placed on top of the bulwarks, and a small *gracht* was built inside the wall with a larger one constructed outside. Amsterdam thus received its present shape of a half-moon.

Up to the expansion, Amsterdam had been a river city along the Amstel with a small front to the IJ. Now it turned its broadest side to a new harbor. The three large *grachts* had more space between them than customary. It therefore became possible to build larger and more spacious houses. Canals joined the *grachts*, and side streets were indispensible for transporting goods. In the new area there was a tendency for the wealthy to separate their dwellings from their warehouses. The plots offered for sale were deep but narrow. Demand and price tended to limit the front side of each house as it faced the *gracht* to a width of three windows, and a house such as the one built with a five window frontage at 123 Keisersgracht was exceptional. Another favorite area for patrician homes was on the Kloveniersburgwal just east and south of the Warmoesstraat.

The stone and brick period in Amsterdam building began about 1600. Before then houses, bridges, and even fortifications had been made of oak. The first stone houses had simple peaked roofs with a triangular *truitgevel* facing the street. Soon this type gable was reserved for rear façades and warehouses as the tastes of the time demanded something more decorative. It was replaced by the stepped gable (*trapgevel*), which looked like a pair of stairs rising to a single flat step. Numerous large blocks of white natural stone were placed along the edges of the gables and windows, in the arches, and on the steps. Set into the façade was a white stone with the date of construction and the name of the original owner. An excellent example of this type of architecture is Rembrandt's house. Remaining in general use up to about 1700, these façades were popular on the small back streets where the middle class lived.

Growing out of the stepped gable was the popular neck gable (*halsgevel*). A small step on each side of the bottom of the gable was covered by decorative designs such as claws. On each step was a tall step to the top, which was crowned with a pediment. In vogue after 1650 was the bell gable (*klokgevel*). It looked like an inverted bell with cartouches, obelisks, Dutch C scrolls, and other decorations at the bottom with additional ornamentation at the top.

The wealthy, however, were turning to the Italian classic with a square façade topped by either a crest or a balustrade. The first house of this type was built by Jacob van Campen (1597–1657) at 177 Keisersgracht. Constructed about 1630, it was a two-family dwelling as was the better known Trip home built by Philips Vingboons (1608–71), architect to the wealthy. Trip's façade was so broad that his footman said he would be perfectly content with a house as wide as Trip's door. His wish was granted. At 26 Kloveniersburgwal, next to his own, Trip built his footman the narrowest house in Amsterdam.

No matter what the façade, it contained some identification mark. A house on the Herengracht proudly displayed a Negro's head on each side of the elaborate doorway to indicate that the money that paid for the house was from the slave trade. All façades but the classical carried a boom with block and tackle jutting out from the gable because narrow stairways prohibited the passage of bulky objects. Homes with warehouses on the top leaned slightly outward to facilitate hoisting.

The larger houses in Amsterdam had four big rooms on the ground floor—two in front and two in back—plus entrance hall, corridor, and stairwell. The entrance hall floor consisted usually of contrasting black and white tiles. Each floor ordinarily had the same number of rooms as could be found on the ground floor. No great house was complete without a rear garden with accompanying pavilion or summerhouse. As the century progressed the more wealthy spent the warmer months in the country.

Walls and ceilings might be elaborately painted with the scenes done directly on the panels or upon canvas fastened to the walls. Heavy ornate furniture, fancy grill-work especially on the stairs and windows, paintings, richly carved mantels, and stucco reliefs filled to varying degrees most of the homes. Door frames abounded with ornamentation ranging from swags to cupids. Each lower class aped the tastes of the group above it. Dutch artists provide a living record of Dutch interiors. Dutch wall beds, heavy furniture, carpeted table covers, walls hung with sometimes garish paintings, brass utensils, dull pewter, and Delftware are familiar objects to students of Dutch artists, especially Jan Steen and Adriaan Ostade. About the beds one tourist remarked that they were dangerous to fall out of, "but if you die in it, this comfort you shall leave your friends that you dy'de in clean linnen."

The interiors were spotless, but Dutch neatness was not always appreciated. The English diplomat, Sir William Temple, was extremely uneasy during a state dinner party because every time he spit on the floor it was wiped up. When he complained, the host said that it was well that his wife was not there for she would have kicked him out of the house. In a similar vein, Feltham wrote: "... you must either go out to spit, or blush when you see the Mop brought." To him Dutch doors appeared studded with diamonds, and "their houses they keep cleaner than their bodies; their bodies than their souls."

The citizens' daily routine varied according to social position. Upper- and middle-class families arose early, washed, and went downstairs. The head of the house or one of the children read from the ever-available Bible, which was heavily bound with brass or copper locks. Breakfast usually consisted of bread, butter, cheese, and beer. Having eaten, the master of the house went to his office, warehouse, wharf, or study, or perhaps to the Exchange or a market place. The children went to school while the wife directed the servants, chatted with the neighbors, or ran the shop if it was connected with the dwelling. Visitors were amazed how well Dutch women handled commercial matters, and it was quite customary for a widow to continue the family business. The status of women was so advanced that foreigners often considered Amsterdam society to be matriarchal.

The big meal was at midday. It could range from the meager fare of much bread and little meat seen in the painting by Nicholas Maes (1632–93), "Our Daily Bread," to the overloaded tables portrayed by the genre painters. The Dutch loved food. They were called "butterboxes" because of "the great quantity of butter eaten," and the term "bumpkin" was probably first used as a name for Dutchmen, meaning a man with a short stumpy figure.

Critics charged that the Dutch overate and drank, came to the table with dirty hands, and grunted and slurped throughout the meal. Thomas Nash has one of his characters say: ". . . the eighth is Foxe drunke, when he is craftie drunke, as many of the Dutch men bee."

The food was hardy, consisting of beef, lamb, mutton, and pork for the rich, and for the middle class, rabbit, fowl, and turkey. In addition, there were beets, salad greens, carrots, and parsnips from Hoorn, rapes, rice pudding, assorted kinds of fresh water fish such as smelt, perch, carp, roach, bream, plus saltwater fish such as herring, haddock, and cod. In the winter the choice was more limited. The poorer classes ate salt fish, dried peas, cheese, bacon, and all sorts of wursts. Those who could afford it had meat throughout the year. Beer was drunk at all noon meals with wine reserved for special occasions. The latter was often served highly spiced. The ladies of Amsterdam loved to stuff themselves with liquor-filled candies and other sweets as they puffed away on their pipes.

The evening meal was often leftovers. A common night meal was a soup called *kouwerschaal* or *bierenbrod*, which consisted of bread and beer sometimes laced with sugar. In good weather this was served in the garden house or outside in the courtyard illuminated by the quiet light of the long summer twilight. A nightcap of gin, wine, or beer was usually consumed at least by the head of the household before the retiring hour of nine o'clock.

No matter what the dish, Dutch cooking was not popular. One visitor readily admitted that the Amsterdamers had an abundance of soups and "Slops," but complained that they boiled or roasted everything "all to Rags, so that you don't know what sort of Flesh 'tis when it come to the Table." By contemporary European standards there was an abundance of food, and the traveler if he took care could eat well and reasonably at the "Ordinaries." Furthermore, many charitable institutions saw to it that the less fortunate received proper care.

Meals at guild meetings, shooting-guild (*schutterij*) banquets, weddings, betrothals, reception of dignitaries, or other special occasions could be sumptuous. The rooms were festooned with greens and flowers, and the number of courses might reach double figures. The entertainment could run from fireworks to music. Hans Bontemantel (1613–88) described a party given by Rembrandt's Dr. Nicholass Tulp (1593–1674) with which Tulp celebrated his fiftieth year as a member of the *Vroedschap*, the governing group of the city. The dinner began at 2:00 P.M., and each guest came provided with his own servant. There were no seating arrangements, and toast after toast was drunk throughout the festivities. Between the twelve courses, there were readings of Latin poems composed especially for the occasion. While listening to these the guests smoked or nibbled at candies and tasty jams. The last drink for the road was served just before 11:00 P.M.

The guests on their way home, if not too befuddled, might have contemplated the great changes that had taken place during Tulp's lifetime. He was born not long after 1578—the year of the Alteratie when Amsterdam declared for Orange—and the party was being held in 1672, the year William III became stadtholder. Tulp's commission to Rembrandt had made the young artist famous overnight. Rembrandt was dead, and the city was becoming increasingly French, especially in architecture. But what a tremendous outpouring of Dutch Renaissance construction had been accomplished—so much that Jan Wagenaar (1700–93), a Dutch Procopius, was to write the history of Amsterdam from its buildings.

The growing city had demanded admiralty buildings, naval docks, and new fortifications. The elaborate design of city gates carried over into domestic portals. The Reformation brought a need for new churches and chapels, and business required a new exchange, new banks, new warehouses, new quarters for the India companies, and new guild halls. A larger Accijnhuis was constructed to facilitate trade in beer, grain, and other commodities. The town fathers who likened themselves to Roman senators tried to emulate the building program of Imperial Rome.

The poets praised the new buildings and artists painted them. Engravers such as Rembrandt with their love for the detailed line preserved them for posterity. Vondel continually sang the praises of his Amsterdam, which he held to be the hub of the world. The center of that hub was the City Hall, from which the town fathers of the city directed the destinies not only of Amsterdam but of large segments of the world.

CHAPTER TWO

The House the Heeren Built

THE GREAT CITY HALL of Amsterdam designed by Jacob van Campen and Daniel Staelpaert was completed in 1655. Its style was Italian Renaissance, but in spirit and construction it was Amsterdamish. As Katharine Freemantle points out, it was conceived "as a statement, made in visual terms but comparable to a vast oration concerning the city's history and status, its civic life, and the ideals of its government." A visitor to the city considered it "a most noble and magnificent Pile of Building. . . . 'tis the stateliest Piece we ever saw; 'tis the Wonder of the World, the Pride of *Amsterdam* and the Glory of the Seven Provinces." Its baroque design, its architectural and sculptural form, and its symbolic decorations expressed more clearly than its makers could have realized the relation of the building to its surroundings and its use. It was the meeting place of the burghers and the seat from which the *Heeren* (the town fathers) directed the destinies of the city.

Amsterdam's form of government was remarkable because the constitution which evolved in the Middle Ages remained actively in operation up to 1795. By the time of the Alteratie (1578), the city was governed by a sheriff (*schout*) who represented the Count of Holland, four burgomasters, nine aldermen, and thirty-six members of the City Council. The entire administration was referred to as either the *Vroedschap* or *Heeren*, that is, the Regents. The burgomasters, who had power "next to God and the Prince," worked through a number of commissions or colleges whose members they appointed. Colleges in charge of taxation, the care of orphans, and the treasury existed before 1578. The latter shortly thereafter was divided into two colleges and was soon to be assisted by a College of Auditors. Also dealing with financial matters were the Commission for the Exchange Bank (1614), the Commission for the Loan Bank (1614), the Insurance Commission (1598), the Commission for Maritime Affairs (1641), and the Bankruptcy Commission (1644). Rembrandt was among the citizens who appeared before the last-named college.

The burgomasters and the aldermen were concerned with all facets of Amsterdam life. The College of Domestic Squabbles published marriage banns, performed the ceremony for those not of the Reformed Church, heard servant complaints, labor disputes and domestic rows, and arbitrated all sorts of trivial matters. Another legal trash bin was the College of Petty Affairs. The men who sat on these legal colleges were either incumbent or former aldermen. Almost none had technical training in law, and their methods did little to charm European legal experts. It is surprising that this administration of justice by amateurs worked as well as it did.

In theory the City Council held the reins of power and had the right to advise, resolve, and dispose of all matters concerning city, province, or country. One historian has pointed out that the council sitting in the City Hall often decided policy for the entire United Provinces—or States as they were called in England. This is at best a half-truth. The method by which the burgomasters were chosen made them wholly independent of the council, and in all matters not specifically designated by law to the colleges, the burgomasters had complete freedom of action. The *Vroedschap* was not entirely subservient or insignificant, but, as Professor Brugsman has so clearly stated, "the tiller of the shipt of state was in the steady hands of the burgomasters."

The burgomasters convened the Council and controlled its agenda, limiting the Council usually to matters dealing with finance which demanded Council approval. Council meetings were often summary, and burgomasters frequently withheld documents pertinent to vital questions. Thus members were forced to make quick decisions based on insufficient information. Appointments made by the Council such as the offices of sheriff and advocate (*pensionaris*) were made on the recommendations of the burgomasters, who had a strong voice in the selection of Council members and in the membership of the various colleges. The burgomasters sat in the Council and had the power to expel Council members who in their opinion committed political or other transgressions.

The burgomasters could be found in every byway of public service. Along with the sheriff and aldermen, they formed the College of the Masters of Justice, which promulgated the city's laws and regulations. Again the Council had reserved to it the lawmaking power, but actually it had little to say. The burgomasters in the name of the Regents published legal decrees and regulations, preserved law and order, and supervised the sheriff. Along with the Treasury they had the sole power to assess fines, and no one could be put to death or banished without burgomaster consent.

Amsterdam's armed forces were also subject to the burgomasters who often in addition to their political duties held commissions in the military guilds (*schutterij*). The guilds played a noteworthy role in Amsterdam life because they included burghers not in the *Vroedschap*, and because in a city where the police was weak, they formed a force sufficient to carry out government policy. At various times the *schutterij* curbed social unrest and preserved law and order. Armed with pike and musket they guarded the city's walls, gates, and bridges, went on campaigns outside the city, and stood watch against natural catastrophes such as flood and fire. They were ready to parade on any occasion and Rembrandt in the "Night Watch" portrayed the company of Captain Frans Banning Coq on display. They commissioned artists to decorate their archery halls (*doelens*), and their banquets were among the city's more important social events.

By Rembrandt's time the guildsmen were better in the social room than on the battlefield. The poet Gerbrand Adriaensz. Bredero (1585–1618) has left pen portraits of his military colleagues. His colonel needed "only to see beer foaming in the glasses to report for duty," his lieutenant could drink his "brimful glasses, even while kissing and cuddling," his standard bearer was "a habitual drunkard," and his pimply corporal never "sheds nor shoots. But he does not step aside when it comes to drinking."

With restrictions, the burgomasters also controlled the Admiralty of Amsterdam, which was one of three naval forces in the Province of Holland and one of five in the United Provinces. The States General technically delegated powers to each admiralty, but the five often worked at cross purposes. The chief income for the naval forces came from duties levied on trade. For the most part each admiralty received the funds raised in the territory under its jurisdiction. Additional revenue came from convoy and licensing fees. Consequently the burgomasters were often more concerned with the convoying of trade than with the defense of national interests. Sometimes the Admiralty of Amsterdam was more involved in the city's foreign and naval policies than in those of the States, and orders from the City Hall were obeyed rather than those from the Hague.

Amsterdam's trading, commercial, and guild life was also supervised by the burgomasters, who named the directors to such companies as the East India Company and operated the postal system at a time when the news of a ship arrival or a political upheaval had repercussions on the Exchange. They held the seal of the city, took care of the city archives, and nominated themselves heirs in perpetuity to manors which were municipal property.

They were the political power behind the state church and the custodians of ecclesiastical wealth. The Reformed Church had formed the Amsterdam classis in 1578, but even in the heat of the moment had been forced to move slowly against the Catholics. At times the discipline could be real, and once a burgomaster came under the lash of the divines. Usually, as in the case of Rembrandt's mistress,

Hendrickje Stoffels, it was little more than spiteful censure.

Amsterdam's religious atmosphere was the wonder of its friends and the dismay of some of its enemies. In describing his native city Remonstrant Minister Geraert Brandt (1626–85) said:

> They [the town fathers] countinence only Calvinism, but for Trade's sake they *Tolerate* all others, except the Papists; which is the reason why the treasure and stock of most Nations is transported thither, where there is full Liberty of Conscience: you may be what Devil you will there, so you be but peaceable; for Amsterdam is an University of all Religions, which grow confusedly (like stocks in a *Nursery*) without either order or pruning. If you be unsettled in your Religion, you may try all, and take at last what you like best; if you fancy none, you have a Pattern to follow of them that would be Church to themselves: It's the Fair of all the Sects, where all the Pedlars of Religion have leave to vend their Toyes, their Ribbands, and Phanatique Rattles; their Republic is more to them than Heaven; and God may be more safely offended there than the States General.

Even the lot of the Roman Catholics was not too burdensome, relatively speaking. An open church was illegal, but in 1656 there were at least sixty-six meeting places where Mass was being celebrated and between fifteen thousand and sixteen thousand Catholics in the city. Later in the century Sir William Brereton noted that Catholics were numerous in Amsterdam where they had "foursome and five Chapels or Mass-Rooms, have no Bills allow'd 'em, are oblig'd to have their Doors always open, and are tolerated as all others are here. They have a large Square of Houses for their Religious to live, but not to be cloister'd up in, who have a Liberty to go, or stay at Pleasure; and to live singly, or to be married, which they like best." John Locke in his *Essay on Toleration* did not go so far as did the burgomasters who governed the city wherein the work first appeared. The *Heeren* under the roof of their baroque City Hall recognized that they could accommodate many mansions.

Even when a burgomaster was not in office, he wielded considerable influence. He sat with other former burgomasters in the Council of Elders, which was consulted on all important matters, not the least of which being the selection of new burgomasters. There was nearly as much prestige in being an ex-burgomaster as there was in being an incumbent. The patricians' policy of keeping the governing class as restricted as possible led to many ex-burgomasters being returned to office after a passage of time. Andries Bicker (1586–1652) held the title on ten separate occasions. There was a real validity to the old Amsterdam saying, "Once a burgomaster always a burgomaster."

Because of the loose organization of the Dutch government, the arm of Amsterdam burgomasters reached beyond the city limits. At one time it was said that the Devil ran the United Provinces because he had the Bicker maid under his spell. Like many Dutch servants she controlled her mistress, who controlled Andries, who controlled Amsterdam, which controlled the Estates of Holland, which controlled the States General—the governing body of the United Provinces. Metaphysics ignored, Amsterdam's "Great Sons" such as Andries Bicker did direct the course of events not only in the States but at times in remote corners of the world as the proud city enforced its will on the rest of the country. Much Dutch history is traceable to the manipulations of the *Heeren* who sat in the new City Hall that they built or in its Flemish predecessor.

From the Alteratie to the twelve-year truce made with Spain in 1609, the *Heeren* had worked with relative harmony with the stadtholder, Prince Maurice of Nassau (1567–1625), and the Grand Pensionary of Holland, John van Oldenbarnevelt (1547–1625). However, the truce brought Amsterdam and the Prince into a sharp conflict with the Estates of Holland and the Grand Pensionary. A large number of Flemish and Brabantine refugees in Amsterdam, who like Prince Maurice were irredentists, considered the desertion of the Southern Netherlands a betrayal to the cause and ideals for which many had suffered and died. Among this group with weath and political power were Willem Usselincx, colonial promoter, and Petrius Plancius, geographer and ardent Calvinist theologian. In addition, the *Heeren* of Amsterdam feared that a truce would end Dutch trade to the Indies and lucrative privateering activities. It would also stop a proposed West India Company for which Usselincx and others envisioned a glowing future. Consequently the truce led to a whispering campaign against Oldenbarnevelt that accused him of everything from accepting Spanish money to being a traitor to country and religion. The truce was to be the old pensionary's Achilles heel.

The influx of South-Netherlanders had led to demands

for a stricter church, but heretofore in Amsterdam and in other major cities the Libertine governments had steered a middle course. In rural areas and among the nonruling classes in the cities, however, the Calvinist majority continually called for tighter discipline and a national synod. Into a touchy situation had come Jacob Arminius, who in 1588 had been called to an Amsterdam pulpit. From the beginning he held views protested by Plancius and others who felt that the Libertines were opening the gates to Roman Catholicism. The attacks of Arminius on sancrosant Calvinist beliefs stirred up a hornet's nest, and consequently Cornelis Hooft, a Libertine burgomaster, worked with others to have the controversial preacher transferred to a theology chair at the University of Leiden. The result was that an Amsterdam ecclesiastical hassle became a national one.

At Leiden, Arminius gathered a group of followers, the best known being Johannes Uyttenbogaert, who became the group leader after the death of Arminius in 1609. Franciscus Gomarus led the Leiden opposition. In 1610 the Libertines presented their views to the States General in a Remonstrant to be answered by a Contra-Remonstrant the following year. There can be little doubt that Oldenbarnevelt and the Estates worked to give the Remonstrant group every legislative advantage. In many ways they were as bigoted as the Calvinists. The battle lines were drawn; the Libertines, to succeed, had to control the cities. The military guilds were Calvinist and could and did oppose the town fathers. The key city in the struggle was Amsterdam, where personal animosities merged with political, and where the economics of a truce haunted Oldenbarnevelt's religious objectives.

The struggle in Amsterdam centered around two personalities, Cornelis Hooft and Reynier Pauw. The former was from an old and respected Calvinist family with many connections, but Cornelis was a man of principle who loved both political and religious freedom. A wealthy merchant and trader, he found time to be a burgomaster and served in that capacity with dignity and honor. He was the friend of the religious refugee. He held that violence begot violence and that no man had the right to use force to impose his convictions upon another. To Hooft, war and quarrels contributed only to godlessness. Like Erasmus and Dirk Coornhert, he appealed to reason and moderation at a time when passions ran high. He was too easygoing and latitudinarian to buck successfully an opposition with rigidly defined goals.

The leader of that opposition, Reynier Pauw, has been considered along with Bicker to be one of Amsterdam's two most typical burgomasters. Merchant and shipowner he represented the trading-company, title-seeking burgher. He supported city expansion programs, was among the initial investors in both India companies, was knighted by England and France, and gave to the office of *magnificat* (head burgomaster) real significance. Violent, purposeful, and dedicated Calvinist, Pauw thrived on political strife. Under his leadership the city enjoyed leaping growth and prosperity. He had old scores to settle with Oldenbarnevelt, and when opportunity presented itself he closed accounts.

By the time that the fight between Remonstrant and Contra-Remonstrant became violent, Pauw controlled the Amsterdam Council by a small majority and all four burgomasters were Contra-Remonstrant. When in 1613 the

States General passed a resolution favoring the Remonstrant minority and calling for ecclesiastical peace, Amsterdam was restless. Plancius and the preacher Jacob Trigland stirred up the populace, and the city refused to sanction the resolution in the Estates of Holland. When the latter moved against Contra-Remonstrants, Pauw and his followers "called on faithful Israel to take arms against the children of Belial."

In April, 1616, Oldenbarnevelt sent a delegation headed by Grotius to Amsterdam hoping to win the City Council over to his cause. Hooft pleaded the cause of the Estates eloquently and using history as an example warned against the dangers of religious strife. Neither the appeals of the "old gentleman" nor the arguments of the legal genius carried any weight. Pauw had the votes and intended to use them. Amsterdam not only declared its intent to resist the resolution, but offered to reimburse Contra-Remonstrant ministers who came into trouble with the provincial and national authorities and threatened to deduct expenses from the city's annual contribution to the national revenues. The City Council in addition offered asylum to Calvinist ministers banished from other Dutch towns.

In Amsterdam a steady stream of pamphlets were directed against the Remonstrants, the best known being one by Trigland entitled *Clear and Fundamental Contra-Remonstrant*. No holds were barred. No bitter terms withheld. No scurrilous phrase or name unused. The Remonstrants had overstepped themselves and did not know how to retreat. The Reformed Church knew its goal—the destruction of the enemy—whereas Uyttenbogaert gave his followers at best only a fuzzy leadership.

At the Hague, Oldenbarnevelt in April, 1617, tried to

take over the army and to use it against his opposition. The troops, however, were loyal to Maurice, who was besieged by petitions from the outlying provinces and James I of England to call a national synod to restore religious peace. The forces of Oldenbarnevelt could not maintain order and the States General over the Pensionary's wishes agreed to call a national synod.

In the early days of the next year the Prince used his powers of appointment to replace Remonstrant magistrates with Contra-Remonstrants. This led to a new outbreak of pamphlet warfare with over 150 coming from the presses. Caricatures and lampoons—mostly anonymous—written in the most bitter language spewed out of the book and print shops of Amsterdam. Some half-hearted attempts were made to punish the most libelous authors and printers, but Pauw and the burgomasters were more interested in Oldenbarnevelt's destruction than in his rights. One of the most violent, *A Necessary and Lively Discourse*, went through at least five printings within the year, and Pauw himself may have been one of the authors, although Trigland or Willem Baudartius seems a more suitable candidate for that dubious honor.

On August 25, 1618, Oldenbarnevelt, Grotius, and Rombout Hogerbeets, pensionary of Leiden, were arrested. Pauw sat as one of the judges in their trials. Oldenbarnevelt went to the block while Grotius and Hogerbeets received prison sentences. The city of Amsterdam had paid off an old score. The national synod held at Dort was as partisan and bigoted as the judges who tried Oldenbarnevelt. Plancius and Trigland led the group that drove all opposition to the ground. The Remonstrants were gagged for a time, but still they existed. The Calvinists gained control of the city's educational system for a time, but failed to set up a church order. With the end of the truce, Pauw got his West India Company, but the *Vroedschap* as a whole still remained Libertine.

From May 12, 1619, the date of Oldenbarnevelt's execution, to 1631, when Andries Bicker and Jacob de Graeff were elected burgomasters, the Calvinists controlled Amsterdam, yet the church never had the strength it enjoyed in other cities. It was not consulted on political matters, and if a Reformed policy was followed it was because the burgomasters had practical reasons. When their power was at its zenith, the intellectuals battled the establishment, led in the fray by Vondel and Bredero. The former, in his play *Palamedes*, most unsubtly reminded Amsterdamers of the judicial murder of Oldenbarnevelt, while Samuel Coster used the theater to attack the Calvinists. Before 1631 the Vroedschap had asserted its right to decide on religious matters, and had expelled two of the most turbulent Reformed preachers from the city. In addition the new stadtholder, Prince Frederick Henry, had Remonstrant leanings and was happy to provide the *Heeren* with a garrison which was used to keep the Calvinist lower classes in order. After 1631 there was little doubt that the town fathers made the city's religious decisions. Amsterdam's patricians had cut the claws of the clergy just as they had those of Oldenbarnevelt and the Estates of Holland. In both cases the Prince had played an important role in the action. The city's next battle would be between the city and the Stadtholder.

In the beginning the two had gotten along famously. Amsterdam backed the Captain-General and furnished him the means to bring about his continuing string of victories against Spain. On the other hand, the city profited economically from Dutch arms. When out of the military successes there began to emerge the possibility of a powerful ruling house and a hereditary monarchy, Amsterdam became first lukewarm and eventually hostile toward the Prince. It was to be Bicker who was to be the champion of the city, just as it was De Graeff who postponed the conflict. The marital ties between the two would require elaborate genealogical tables. Bicker was De Graeff's nephew by marriage and two of De Graeff's daughters married Bickers. The two highly interrelated families represented a new group of regents united by blood and marriage, who for the most part held the reins of government in their hands up to 1672.

De Graeff was typical of the Amsterdam of his time. He loved the city and reveled in his country place, from which he took the title Vrijheer van Zuid-Polsbroed and where he bred hunting dogs. He had a keen interest in philosophy and natural science, and had studied the classics at Leiden under Professor Rudolph Snellius. In addition he had made the Grand Tour with the famous Justius Lipsius. An amateur musician, businessman, bank director, regent, and cultured gentleman, De Graeff died a shining example of the *Heeren* at his home on the Herengracht. Vondel commented: "De titel maakt alleen geen Graef." ("The title alone does not make a count.")

De Graeff had been a member of the *Vroedschap* from 1603 to 1618, when he had been stripped of his offices because of his loyalty to Oldenbarnevelt. De Graeff never forgave Pauw for his role against the Pensionary but did remain loyal to Prince Maurice. A chair now in the Rijksmuseeum was highly cherished by the De Graeff family because in it Prince William himself had sat while dining with the family. This loyalty to the House of Orange by the De Graeffs was to serve Prince William's descendents well throughout much of the seventeenth century. In religion as in politics, Jacob de Graeff steered a middle road. He was a friend to Uyttenbogaert and other Remonstrants, but held firmly to the Calvinist doctrine of predestination. The year of his death 1638 marks the beginning of open hostilities between Frederick Henry and Amsterdam led by Andries Bicker and his friends.

Bicker was "Mr. Burgomaster" incarnate. His grandfather's brewery was the basis of the family fortune, and his father, burgomaster and member of the *Vroedschap* among other posts, established the family politically. Andries and his three brothers practically divided the trade of the world among themselves. Andries trafficked in India spices and Russian furs. Jacob imported Baltic grain, and Cornelis turned his attentions to America and had a good deal of capital invested in the West India Company when Piet Heyn made his highly profitable capture of the Spanish silver fleet. Jan traded to the Levant and built ships. Family interests rather than jealousies dominated the thinking of the four. Vondel was hardly indulging in poetic license when he wrote:

> *The great sea shaded by the Bicker flag,*
> *Over richly laden ships unfurled,*
> *Cutting waves to lay in Holland's bosom*
> *The golden treasures of the world.*

The political arena belonged to Andries, not because he was the eldest but because he was the most able. The second position belonged to Cornelis.

The struggle of the "Bicker League" with the Stadt-holder began in 1638. Frederick Henry wished to conquer the Southern Netherlands and unite the Low Countries. Antwerp was the key to his dream. Once that city was under the Orange banner, the Scheldt could be open to navigation. A revitalized Antwerp would balance the financial monopoly of Amsterdam and free the Prince in war, trade, politics, and diplomacy from the tutelage of the Amsterdam burghers.

As Antwerp became more elusive of his design for capture, Frederick Henry's pique toward Amsterdam increased. No fool, he knew that Amsterdam and other Holland merchants were illegally providing the beleagured Antwerpers with ships and supplies, that Amsterdamers had convoyed the Spanish silver fleet to the South Netherlands so that the Spanish soldiers could be paid, and that enemy privateers out of Dunkirk and Ostend were carrying on a thriving business with Amsterdam merchants in loot and war booty. In addition, Bicker and two other burgomasters were in the process of building along the Zuider Zee ships destined for Spanish service. Consequently a commission from the States General was sent in 1639 to Amsterdam. It hoped that a local desire to break the "Bicker League" might tempt the *Vroedschap* to decide against the three guilty burgomasters. Except for a sham formal meeting, the delegation did not even have a hearing. The first round in the bout between Mister Burgomaster and Prince Stadtholder went to Mijnheer Bicker.

Throughout the 1640's the power struggle continued. As Frederick Henry's son had married the daughter of Charles I, the Prince wanted to aid the Stuarts. Amsterdam opposed this as it had the Antwerp adventure. The *Heeren* were more interested in Northern Europe than in either the South Netherlands or Great Britain. There Sweden and Denmark were again at war. Amsterdam thought that the time was ripe to break Denmark's control of the Baltic Sea. Especially onerous was a Danish tax on every ship entering or leaving the Baltic. Technically these "Sound dues" were to aid navigation. Actually they were an out-and-out levy made possible because Denmark held land on both sides of the Sound. Dutch shippers, whose vessels constituted more than half of those passing the Sound, considered the tax to be little more than tribute.

Some Amsterdamers had personal motives. Andries Bicker was in the Baltic fur trade; his brother Jacob in the grain trade. Of greater economic magnitude were the widespread activities of Louis de Geer, whose financial and business transactions raised him from Amsterdam burgher to Swedish peer. De Geer at this time owned and operated the famous Swedish iron mines which supplied much of Western Europe. In addition, he operated a world-wide business in armaments. The center of his financial empire was Amsterdam. The Trip family had even more important trade and business concessions in Sweden. In addition, during the Spanish war Amsterdamers had found time and money to provide Sweden with an entire battle fleet, which was used with telling success against the Danes.

The States General sent two envoys to the Baltic, one being Andries Bicker. They returned with a proposal that the Dutch intervene in the Baltic struggle on Sweden's behalf. This provision was pushed in the States General by the States of Holland prodded by Amsterdam and was contradictory to the Orange-Stuart policy, which favored Denmark. The Prince's hands were tied. Holland held the purse strings and controlled three out of five of the admiralties. Any Dutch diplomacy, be it British, Baltic, or Antwerpian, depended on money and sea-power.

Violent scenes took place between the states of Holland and the Prince as Bicker and Jacob de Witt of Dort pushed the anti-Danish policy. Frederick Henry was forced to give way. A strong fleet of Dutch merchantmen under convoy forced the Sound without paying the customary dues while the Danish court and people watched helplessly from the shore. Like the Stadtholder they had to bow to Holland's naval preponderance. The commander of the squadron, Witte de Witt, had been instructed to avoid open hostilities; still, the demonstration led to a new Dano-Dutch treaty. The Hollanders had to tone down some of their demands regarding the Sound dues, because Frederick Henry was able to convince enough members of the States that national policy dictated friendly relations with Denmark.

Although the hopes of the Stuarts had been shattered at Naseby, Frederick Henry late in 1645 and early 1646 tried to equip a fleet in Amsterdam to aid his in-laws. He was unsuccessful. The city still feared the Prince's ambitions regarding Antwerp, and strong anti-Roman Catholic feeling in the city prevented any action detrimental to Calvinism. To the Reformed ministers, the policies of the Stuart Archbishop of Canterbury, William Laud, had besmacked of Popery. Catholics might be tolerated in Amsterdam for trade's sake, but that was as far as the *Heeren* would go.

Prince and city were continually at odds over naval administration. The admiralty colleges often connived at wholesale evasion of convoy and licenses dues, and many times the term protection of commerce meant the trade of a specific town rather than Dutch trade on the whole. Attempts made by the States General and the inland provinces to supervise the admiralties came to naught. After all, Amsterdam was hiring its ships out to the enemy, and the burghers involved wanted no check on their activities. The Bickers themselves were implicated. When a debate to investigate such practices was held in the Amsterdam council, the delegates of the Prince were excluded.

In all these events the Bickers had played a leading role. With their in-laws, they had manipulated city and state to a much greater degree than had their predecessors. They commanded the city's garrisons; they directed diplomatic and naval operations in the Baltic. They opened peace negotiations with Spain against the wishes of the Prince. A year before the peace was concluded at Münster, Frederick Henry had died a tired, sick, and disappointed man.

The son and successor, William II, was more forceful than the father. Frederick Henry dreamed of establishing some sort of an hereditary monarchy; William II planned to do so. He had no intention of bowing to the Bickers. He proposed to exercise all his rights and run the Republic. His strength lay with the army. His foes realized this and ever since the peace they had been demanding through the States of Holland a reduction of the armed forces. The frugal burghers of Amsterdam meanwhile had dismissed the city's garrisons at a time when it was rumored that Andries Bicker aspired to replace the Prince as Count of Holland. William II struck. In 1650 he imprisoned some of his political opponents and moved the army of the States General against Amsterdam.

The "Bicker League" prepared for a siege and drew up plans to cut the dikes. The more moderate members of the Council, however, realized what a full-scale siege, the breaking of the dikes, and the stoppage of shipping would do to the city's economic life. Also distressing was the fact that the other cities of Holland showed no inclination to come to Amsterdam's aid. Many of them had been victims of Amsterdam economic and political exploitation. They felt that it was time that the *Heeren* received their comeuppance.

A treaty was drafted on August 3 between William II and Amsterdam. The city promised for the next four or five years to conform to the decisions of the States General regarding military matters, and the Prince agreed to raise his siege of the city. A separate article, which the town fathers sought to escape, stipulated that Andries and Cornelis Bicker step down from office. This round went to the Prince.

The settlement was only a surface truce. In the city the Bickers were considered heroes, patriots, and martyrs. Even those Amsterdamers happy to see the proud Bickers humbled were nevertheless concerned about and opposed to the Prince's interference in Amsterdam politics. Their fears were short lived. On November 6, 1650, the House of Orange suffered a terrible blow. William II died suddenly from smallpox. The only consolation of the stunned Orangists was that eight days later William III, destined to be the stadtholder-king of the Netherlands and Great Britain, was born.

There was real concern throughout the States over the

death of the Prince, because heretofore there had always been a member of the House of Orange to lead the Netherlands in moments of adversity. At the time the anti-Orangists rejoiced; they might cry later as they would in 1672 when young William III would be called upon to turn back the armies of Louis XIV. In 1650, however, one Amsterdamer was so enthusiastic about the turn of events that he enclosed the following with his church offering:

> *The prince deceased*
> *My gift's increased:*
> *No news pleased more*
> *In years four score.*

The leading Bickers too left the scene. Andries died in 1653, and Cornelis a year later.

The Bicker relatives, however, remained an important force in Amsterdam and Netherlandish politics. Cornelis de Graeff, son of Jacob and spouse of a Bicker, became *magnificat* in 1651. Like Andries he was a ten-time burgomaster. He lived on the Herengracht but had a farm on the Soestdijk, which was the forerunner of the present palace. Governing occupied most of his time. He had steered a middle course between William II and the "Bicker League." A defender of the Republic, he stood by the city. Yet he was loyal to the House of Orange and was against scrapping a family that had served the nation so faithfully and so long. His brother's marriage to a Bicker and the fact that Dr. Banningh Coq was an in-law strengthened his position. In addition, his niece Wendela, daughter to Dr. Jan Bicker, married Jan de Witt, who became Grand Pensionary of Holland. The alliance was advantageous to them both and for twenty years they worked together despite disagreements on Baltic diplomacy and on the future role of the House of Orange.

After William II's death, the more radical members of the Holland Estates had hoped to abolish the unique position of the Orangists. They argued that there could be no practical value in the infant William III and that the time was ripe to settle old debts. However, the moderates prevailed. Led by De Graeff and Adriaan Pauw, son of Reynier, they kept the government from going to extremes. The battle was bitter. States fought states, and cities battled cities. In the end it was evident that Amsterdam could no longer thwart the will of the nation.

De Graeff and his followers also toned down the Orangist extremists in Gelderland and Overijssel as well as the anti-Orangists in Holland. During the first Anglo-Dutch war the Orange cause and the national one became fused when Cromwell demanded as a stipulation for peace the repudiation of both Stuart and Orange. After all the mother of William III was the sister of Charles II. When the latter returned home from Dutch Breda in 1660, the hand of the Orange party was strengthened. The De Witt–Cromwell pact to keep Orange and Stuart from power was at least half invalidated. Animosities heightened. De Graeff intervened and invited the dowager princess and her young son to Amsterdam for a five-day visit. During a most lavish entertainment, De Graeff pointed out that the young prince was not ready to assume responsibility. He proposed that the States of Holland appoint a committee to educate William III to the duties of stadtholder, and served on that short-lived body himself.

De Graeff died on May 4, 1664, and henceforth De Witt's relationship with Amsterdam became more strained. The mantle of *magnificat* instead of going to De Graeff's son Andries went to that born intriguer Gillis Valcknier, who during the Second Dutch War had been anti-Orange. By 1670, however, he had moved into the camp of William III. Valcknier's political route—motivated mostly by self-interest—was devious. He tacked with the winds of opportunity.

Unrest in the outlying provinces forced De Witt in 1670 to allow William III, that "child of state," a seat in the national council, but he and the States of Holland managed to keep him out of the States General. By that time Valcknier, a fellow burgomaster of Amsterdam, Conrad van Beuningen, and Caspar Fagel of Haarlem had gone Orange. At one time Van Beuningen had been a close friend of De Witt, but since 1666 a growing coolness had developed between the two as Van Beuningen had tried to follow a middle road between the extremists. De Witt could still count on the Bickers and the De Graeffs. So long as they held Amsterdam, he was secure. But in 1669 the elections had gone against them and their friends. Consequently the recommendations of the Grand Pensionary began to have little or no effect. In the city elections of 1671, the opposition of De Witt to Valcknier, the Trip family, and Van Beuningen drove them and their followers into the Orange fold. Although Valcknier used every political trick to win the burgomaster seats, he failed because of De Witt's interference. Not one of his candidates was elected. De Witt had brought the proud relatives of the Trips and the Pauws down ignominiously. They never forgave him. Andries de Graeff was back in power, but the victory was a Pyrrhic one.

De Witt meanwhile had, by joining in 1668 the Triple

Alliance with England and Sweden, been able to stop the steady advance of France into the Low Countries. By 1672, through bribery and secret diplomacy, Louis XIV weaned away the Dutch allies. The United Provinces stood alone. The "Sun King" was out for revenge. He did not take to base-born burghers thwarting his schemes for grandeur. The States were ill prepared. The army, neglected for years, was not even cohesive because De Witt had systematically cut up the troops into provincial units. Staggering sums were necessary to put the forces into any sort of fighting shape. There was also the question of command. William III, now twenty, by custom and by the will of the majority was the logical leader. Whenever the Dutch were in dire straits, they turned Orange. Threats to Dutch security and the war closed the door on the attempts of De Witt and the anti-Orange party to exclude the boy prince from what the bulk of his countrymen considered to be his rightful place.

Amsterdam was the logical target for the victorious French armies sweeping through the Low Countries. The city debated cutting the dikes. Andries de Graeff prepared the city for a siege and burgomaster Cornelis Hop rallied the citizens. Then came word from The Hague. The disgruntled citizens there had pulled De Witt and his brother from the prison they were in for treason and had torn them to pieces. The States of Holland pressured by events and the mob raised William III on July 4, 1672 to the stadtholdership and made him captain-general of the armies. Amsterdam concurred, and William III by cutting the dikes was able to save Holland from the French.

The city, however, paid a price. The Prince proclaimed the right to have his own followers govern the city during the emergency. As a result, Valcknier, his toadies, and his relatives returned to office. From 1672 to 1680, Valcknier was *magnificat*, and pretty much the sole ruler of Amsterdam. By that time the high-water mark of the city had been reached, but the ebb was not very noticeable. The decline was relative. Amsterdam's primacy simply gave way to London and Paris.

The regents of Amsterdam have at times been treated with undue harshness. They, however, were not a group apart, and the City Hall with its beautiful Hall of the Burghers was accessible to all. Understandably certain wealthy burghers not on the inside wanted a say in civic affairs. Yet this group had no desire to push matters to extremes, because under the rule of the *Heeren* the city enjoyed its greatest period of growth and prosperity. The Regents for their part were relatively moderate. Before 1672 there was no sharp cleavage between the governing and the governed. The two worked together; not always in perfect harmony, but together. Without all of the closely defined verbiage of modern constitutionalism, the *Vroedschap* represented the spirit and the aspirations of the Amsterdamers.

Civic pride is as important as democracy. It was a sense of community that built the orphanages and old peoples' homes as well as the great buildings, that built edifices for the lowly as well as for the mighty. Vondel in one of his more bitter poems might have the Regents declare to the public that they were asses created to bear the burdens of society, but for the most part his verse soars in admiration for the town fathers who had made so much prosperity for so many. His dedication to the City Hall showed his esteem for the Regents just as the building itself represented the pride of the citizenry in the city.

The *Heeren* have been accused of greed, nepotism, self-interest, and a host of crimes which seem to be worse when committed by burghers rather than by nobles or stalwarts of the lower classes. Actually there was less malpractice in the City Hall than in the Whitehall of Charles II or the Versailles of Louis XIV. In the nineteenth century the merchant rulers came under fire from Orangists who considered Amsterdam's republicanism to be a threat to the monarchy. In our own time the Marxist and socialist urge to discredit capitalism has molded public opinion against Amsterdam's ruling class during the time of Rembrandt. In the main, however, the *Heeren* produced a number of dedicated public servants, many far above those in present-day city government.

In the beginning of the seventeenth century there was no great separation of power and wealth between the governing group and other well-to-do burghers. Those in the seats of the mighty had sprung from the ranks of brewers, tailors, tanners, and various types of artisan-merchants as their very names indicate. In 1615, Burgomaster Hooft could honestly say that the government consisted entirely of either merchants or persons who at one time had engaged in trade. The *Vroedschap* came from trade and ruled a city dedicated to it. Outsiders might scoff as did Descartes: "In this great town where apart from myself there dwells no one who is not engaged in trade, everyone is so much out for his own advantage that I should be able to live my whole life here without even meeting a mortal being." Still, as Professor Pieter Geyl tells us: "If one begins by recognizing that the policy of an organism such as Amsterdam must attach immense importance to trade, then there remains much in the life and work of its oligarchic exponents that, in the conditions such as they were settled . . . has possessed great positive value for Dutch life."

As the century progressed, the governing class began to invest money in houses, estates, and securities rather than in ships, merchandise, and manufactures. Money accumulated in trade did not return to trade; and the burgher who combined shop and home was no longer to be found among the patrician oligarchy governing the city. The *Heeren* began to cut fine figures in their town houses along the Singel and the three great *grachts*, and they gave themselves titles of nobility after the names of manors which they had purchased in the reclaimed Beemster or on the river Vecht. As Professor Geyl has so aptly put it, many of the leading Amsterdam regents remained businessmen and managed great concerns or at least were directly interested in them, but public office more and more occupied an important place in their lives. Often they trained themselves for public service from youth. Hooft is an excellent example of a man whose civic duty caused him increasingly to devote his time to public affairs. So is Dr. Tulp, who as he grew older gave fewer anatomy lessons and became increasingly involved in municipal affairs.

New men now and then did filter into the governing circle—usually temporarily and not in sufficient numbers for the health of the body politic. On the whole the oligarchy continued in power long after the "golden age." This might not have been so deleterious if self-interest had not blinded the oligarchy to the main concerns of the city. By 1672 the governing groups had turned their backs on the inheritance of Amsterdam—trade and commerce. They also became intolerant. All opposition and unrest was harshly and ruthlessly crushed. Consequently social dissatisfaction in the eighteenth century opened the city gates to the troops of Revolutionary France. The City Hall, symbol of the burghers and artisans of Amsterdam, was converted into a palace, first for the Bonapartes and later for the House of Orange. The house that the *Heeren* built might be the residence of royalty, but nothing can ever separate it from the burgher aristocracy that planned it and built it and the trade of the city that paid for it.

CHAPTER THREE

Market of the World

AMSTERDAM'S SAGA is a most colorful chapter in economic history and urban development. In the eyes of foreigners, the city almost overnight became a boom town. Antoyne de Montchrétien, a French poet and economist, in 1615 called Holland a miracle of economic development and asserted that "the art of industry had made a masterpiece out of nature's miscarriage." The Romans, he said, took three hundred years to control their territories, the Dutch twenty-five. Later the great French financial minister Jean Baptiste Colbert referred to Holland as a "business house." Foreign travelers from all over Europe were astonished at the prosperity of Holland and the phenomenal expansion of Dutch activities in all fields of endeavor. Visitors ranging from English artisan to Russian tzar came from abroad to study Dutch marketing and industrial techniques along with Dutch economic and social institutions.

The Dutch themselves marveled at their own successes, but modestly considered that God was merely rewarding them for the sacrifices they had made on behalf of the true religion during the grim Eighty Years War. One of the mottoes of the Sea Beggars had been: "Help thyself and God will help thee." They had helped themselves—some of their enemies might have added to almost everything. Now God was showing his beneficence. Holland was the most densely populated and the most prosperous area in Europe; the queen city of the province was Amsterdam. Holland might be the "business house," but Amsterdam kept the till and had the most to say on how commercial transactions were handled.

Amsterdam, one-time fishing village, parlayed its fishing activities into a trading and commercial empire. Actually the rise of Amsterdam was not so phenomenal as contemporaries and historians would have us believe. The roots of Amsterdam's trade stretch into the Middle Ages. The city began to play a major role in Baltic trade just about the period when the Hanseatic League began to decline. The movement of the herring schools from the Baltic to the North Sea in the early part of the fifteenth century increased Amsterdam's trade not only in those areas but throughout Roman Catholic Europe. Recent scholarship has shown that the great maritime code of sea laws coming from Visby in the fourteenth century was influenced by a number of similar codes, among them the "Provisions of Amsterdam." Amsterdam a century earlier had received a charter giving it freedom of tolls, as might be expected of a trading town. When in 1489 Maximilian placed the Imperial crown above the seal of the city, he was recognizing that Amsterdam by that time was a place of considerable significance.

In addition to the all important herring, Amsterdamers traded in the Baltic for grain, metals, flax, hemp, pitch, and tar, items which were then sent to France and Portugal for wine and salt. These products admittedly do not have the glamor of "spicerie" and "things of complaisance" found in Venetian galley or Portuguese carvel. They are bulk products, but many of them such as pitch, hemp, and tar, along with timber, were in vital demand in an age of wooden ships and sail. Furthermore, the timber trade, to quote Daniel Defoe, was a "nursery for seamen." When Lodovico Guicciardini wrote so aptly in 1561 about the Low Countries, he admired the wealth of Amsterdam and noted that there were five hundred ships in the harbor. Many of them came from Antwerp, which Guicciardini considered the finest and most advanced city in Europe. So far as the Low Countries were concerned he rated Amsterdam next in importance to Antwerp.

There can be little doubt that the deterioration of Antwerp's trade contributed to the growth of Amsterdam's commerce, especially to the rise of Amsterdam as a money market; but the decline of Antwerp is not the sole explanation for the greater economic superiority which Amsterdam came to enjoy. At the height of its glory Amsterdam was a combined Antwerp and Venice. For that reason the South Netherlanders who left Brabant and Flanders for the North were not all motivated by religious reasons, although with the majority religious persecution was the chief cause for their going. Continual warfare in those provinces had made trade difficult if not impossible. The goods of the market place were seized on land by the Papists and on the seas by the Protestants. Thus many burghers found themselves stranded economically regardless of their religious affiliations. There was no recourse except to leave. Parma—more merciful than modern dictators—allowed the emigrants to take sizeable amounts of money and worldly goods with them. Antwerp's misfortune was Amsterdam's gain.

When the troubles with Spain began, Antwerp was by far the greater city of the two. Amsterdam had no money mart and could not approach the reputation of its future rival. Yet in many ways Amsterdam's trade and commerce rested on a firmer footing. Antwerp was a port without a merchant fleet. The vessels that linked Antwerp with northern and southern Europe belonged either to those far distant lands or to ship owners in Holland or Zeeland, who were already competing with the Hansa. Certain of the North Netherlandish ports had become staples as Amsterdam had become the staple for Baltic grain. As time went on, it was Amsterdam shippers, Amsterdam masters and crews, and Amsterdam merchants that dominated the North Sea and Baltic trades.

Thus it is quite probable that even without the war Amsterdam in time might have outstripped Antwerp as the dominant commercial city in the Low Countries. Still the military actions pushed Amsterdam forward economically. As Burgomaster Hooft was to write later: "It is known to all the world that whereas it is generally the nature of war to ruin the land and people, these countries [the United Provinces] on the contrary have been noticeably improved thereby." Furthermore, Amsterdam was not above using force to advance its trade. She closed the Scheldt River and strangled Antwerp's sea-borne commerce. She used murder and arson to exclude the British from the East Indies and the military to push the Swedes out of Delaware. Amsterdam naval units compelled the Zuider Zee towns to subordinate their own business interests to those of Amsterdam. The double entente of trade and war paid off. Amsterdam became the economic marvel of the century.

Amsterdam owed little to nature for its fantastic commercial prosperity. The city had grown out of a marsh, and the metamorphosis to a "golden swamp with heaven's plentitude replete" was the result of the efforts of man rather than of gifts from geography. Many cities in the Low Countries had better locations. Admittedly the Zuider Zee provided fish and eels but the Amsterdamer had to catch, cure, and market them. And the herring came from the North Sea, the cod from Newfoundland, and the whale oil from the Arctic. On the other hand, nature did give Amsterdam one advantage. Like Venice, the city was relatively easy to defend from the landward side especially if the dikes were cut.

The close alliance between the *Vroedschap* and the business community was a vital factor in Amsterdam's economic success. The commercial life of the city was strictly regulated by the ruling oligarchy, which in many ways was a guild merchant tolerant of foreigners regardless of their religious beliefs or the animosities of local guilds towards them. Up to 1622 it required only eight guilders to become a burgher; after that the fee was raised to fourteen. To the chagrin of natives, the town fathers admitted foreign craftsmen in large numbers, found housing for the strangers, helped them become established, and offered extra rewards if they introduced new trades or improved techniques in older ones. Shipping was expanded to meet current needs; the special courts and other institutions set up by the Regents fostered economic development.

Without its elaborate organization, Amsterdam perhaps never could have profited from or filled to the extent that it did the vacuum resulting from the economic decline of the Hanseatic League, Genoa, Venice, and Antwerp. The Chamber of Assurance was set up in 1598; the East India Company was chartered in 1602; a new bourse was begun in 1608; a special bourse for transactions in grain was begun in 1616; the Exchange Bank was founded in 1609, and the Lending Bank in 1614; the West India Company was chartered in 1621.

Amsterdam fostered numerous explorations to the White Sea and the Black, to Greenland and Surinam, around Cape Horn and around the Cape of Good Hope, to the East Indies and to the West. The Admiralty aided the trader and the trader aided the Admiralty. Often it was difficult to disassociate the two. The ships trading to the East Indies were both freighters and war vessels. These ships sailing out of Amsterdam were owned by local merchants individually or collectively. They carried the products of foreign countries to Amsterdam and then distributed them abroad. They were the "carriers of the world." Antwerp was just the opposite—one great glamorous trading fair. Even before the war with Spain, Amsterdam was through trade fulfilling a cultural role in Europe even though it was not engaged in the luxury market as much as was Antwerp.

The Dutch attitude toward business is extremely important to the development of Amsterdam's world-wide supremacy in trade and commerce. In the first place the Amsterdamer did not hold labor and the products of labor in disdain. These were a practical people who, like Carlyle, believed that "to work was to pray." Their entire penal and poor-relief systems were built on the premise that idle hands make candidates for the devil. Orphans were taught occupations. Young girls from the orphanages, trained in the domestic arts, were in great demand in the East Indies. Older people remained economically active as long as possible. Beggars and vagrants were given short shrift in Amsterdam, and visitors often commented on how few of these "sturdy rogues" they encountered in the city. James Howell wrote: "And yet it is a rare thing to meet with a Beggar here, as rare as to see a horse, they say, upon the *Streets of Venice*; and this is held to be one of their best pieces of Government." Another foreigner remarked on reaching the shipbuilding town of Zaandaam: "Here we saw some few Beggars, and except some Foreigners (most French) at Amsterdam, we met with no Beggars in all our Travels in the Provinces. The Natives chuse to be Out-liers, rather than come to *Amsterdam*, where they shall have Bread, but they must work for it."

There was a side not so pretty. During the period of economic expansion, there was considerable poverty. The situation was probably due to the price revolution, which hiked food and housing costs and which reached its climax in the middle of the seventeenth century. Wages lagged behind prices, and children under the guise of charity were often horribly exploited. Many of the abuses found in England's industrial revolution were prevalent in Rembrandt's Amsterdam. Yet charitable institutions catered to thousands daily giving "bed and board." Contributions to charity were amazingly high, especially considering that Calvinism offered no spiritual rewards for good works.

Most Amsterdamers were trained for some sort of a job either at school, at home, or in the house of a master. Craftsmen took pride in their skills, often a result of family training. The child assisted and learned in the family workshop or business house, and continued with pride the occupation of its ancestors. Youth of both sexes were trained in geometry and arithmetic, along with languages, speech, and business methods. The wives of Amsterdamers because of their education were able to carry on the affairs of their husbands when they were away "as diligently and discreetly as if they were at home." Often when the husband died, the widow preserved the business until the children came of age. Sometimes mother and children formed partnerships. Most women in trade were widows, but many of them did more than hold the fort between their widowhoods and their sons' majorities. Certain of them, such as the widows Deutz., Thibaut, and Rogge, displayed a real acumen and capacity for commerce.

Amsterdam children were taught honesty, ambition, and thrift. Voltaire's, "Amsterdam, canaux, canards, canailles . . . ." was probably spoken in jest. Along with the large supply of merchandise and money Dutch honesty prompted foreigners to come to Amsterdam for goods and loans. Perhaps Dutch thriftiness is associated with the term "Dutch treat." One of the most popular stories for Amsterdam youngsters concerned a modest employee in a goldsmith's shop who asked each evening for the right to clean the floor. Nightly he burned his sweepings and made for himself a small bar of gold or silver which he eventually invested and made a fortune. It is a tale of waste not want not, and it influenced youthful thinking as much as the exploits of Piet Heyn who captured the Spanish silver fleet and whose deeds were celebrated in verses and songs known to all Amsterdam children.

Intelligent taxation and customs policies also aided

Amsterdam's rise to a world mart. New trades were encouraged and often subsidized either by outright grants or freedom of customs. Foreign merchants were given the same trading rights as the free-born, and duties throughout the city were kept at a minimum. The Amsterdamers preferred custom in volume to high excise taxes crippling to trade.

Professor Violet Barbour in her excellent book *Capitalism in Amsterdam in the 17th Century* claims that the economic primacy of Amsterdam had a threefold base. It was a great shipping center; it was a commodity market; it was a market for capital. Shipping along with fishing laid the basis for the other two. The Dutch boom in shipping rested on a number of causes. First the Dutch ships were capable of carrying heavier cargoes than those of their competitors, partly because the historical emphasis had been founded upon the transportation of bulk commodities. Dutch fishing "busses," which could hold larger catches than those of their rivals, made possible the processing of the herring on board ship. Another famous ship type, the flute *(fluit)* appeared just when Amsterdam began to expand commercially. It could carry more cargo, make longer voyages, and was cheaper to operate than many much smaller foreign designs. The ships destined for the East Indian service were also specially constructed.

Fishing and the expanding trade created an acute demand for ships. Although neither the bus nor the flute was originally designed in Amsterdam, the city was a thriving place for shipbuilders. Supplies of hemp, timber, pitch, tar, and flax were more readily available in Amsterdam and at cheaper rates than elsewhere in Europe. Thus Amsterdam shipbuilders had an advantage over other competitors. Eventually Zaandaan surpassed Amsterdam in this activity, but in Rembrandt's time ship construction was an important occupation. When the trade moved to Zaandaan, Amsterdam bankers and merchants maintained a controlling interest.

Between 1580–1604 Amsterdam admitted to citizenship 1,083 persons engaged in shipbuilding or shipping; many came from North Holland and Friesland towns rather than from the South Netherlands. A sawmill invented in the late sixteenth century was in operation in Amsterdam in 1589. When the monopoly of the original owners expired in 1619, sawmills multiplied on the outskirts of the city. The male house of correction called the *Rasphuis* (sawing house) kept prisoners busy preparing timber. The woodsaw millers linked with the corn millers listed 94 people in their guild. Brereton saw excellent windmills four stories high placed alongside of a navigable ditch. These mills were double ones and used at least sixteen saws at a time. They could saw a piece of lumber twenty yards long in less than an hour. As Dr. Simon Hart points out, there were seventy-four sawmills in Amsterdam in 1665. The outfitting of ships was also a big business. The East India Company sometimes employed as many as 1,200 men in this way. They consisted mostly of sailmakers, anchor smiths, and ropemakers.

Ships were built and outfitted for foreigners as well as for Amsterdamers. Sometimes it was for the enemies of Holland. Amsterdam was constantly accused of sending naval stores and ships to such foes as Parma, Philip II, and later Louis XIV of France. The city sold ships and supplies to both belligerents during the wars between Denmark and Sweden, regardless of national policies.

Henry IV and later the French ministers Fouquet and Colbert bought Amsterdam ships. In 1680 the brothers Dirck and Gysberto Mels contracted to build ten warships for the Spanish navy. This traffic in naval stores and ships continued well into the eighteenth century. Actually Amsterdam today still builds and sells ships to foreign buyers.

Governments were not the only customers. Merchantmen in the seventeenth century had to protect themselves at all times, for there was no peace "beyond the line." One might encounter pirates before the line was even reached. Consequently merchants trading far afield needed ships that could defend themselves. They came to Amsterdam for them. The English Muscovy Company chartered Amsterdam ships in 1597 and 1598. At various times the Portuguese purchased Dutch ships for their Brazil trade, and French mercantilists needing ships to build a colonial empire turned to Amsterdam. France, attempting to enter the Indian and the East Indian trade, bought the ships known as East Indiamen at Amsterdam. Admittedly Zaandaan became famous because of its shipyards, and it was there that Peter the Great came in the late seventeenth century to learn the trade. Yet as Professor Barbour states: "Amsterdam was not, of course, the sole Dutch port capable of providing ships, but she had the largest pool of shipping on which to draw, and her yards and storehouses were furnished with materials for turning out and arming ships of fighting strength." So excellent were Dutch ships that Englishmen from Sir Walter Raleigh to Samuel Pepys urged their countrymen to incorporate Dutch designs and techniques into the English shipbuilding program. As for Dutch seamen, they were a drinking, stealing, fighting, brawling lot, but as an Englishman remarked: "A mess of their Knaves are worth a million of ours; for they in a boisterous rudeness can work, and live, and toil, whereas ours will rather laze themselves to poverty."

The perfection of trade techniques contributed both to shipping and to commerce. The exchange system which made Amsterdam the money mart of the world grew up like Uncle Tom's Topsy. Sometime in the city's development the merchants met in a single place—first by chance and later by arrangement. In the early sixteenth century, they gathered in the Warmoesstraat, and on that street an early type of exchange came into existence. By 1561 the customary meeting place was on the Oostzide van het Nieuwe Brug over the Damrak (the east side of the new bridge over the Damrak). On good days they congregated in the street, but when the skies were threatening they moved into St. Olaf's Chapel or the Old Church. Up to 1592 they seem to have met twice a day, but in the seventeenth century a single daily session sufficed. In 1611 the Beurs, located at the end of the Rokin by the Dam, was built under the direction of De Keyser. The new building in the Renaissance style of the day was modeled on the exchanges of Antwerp and London. It was a covered gallery around an open plain, and above the gallery was an arcade where the finest luxury items were sold. This edifice became the center of the Amsterdam staple market and the hub of European commerce.

Actual trading was generally done outside the Beurs: in the burgher room of the City Hall or in the innumerable coffee houses and taverns. The Exchange itself decided questions of price, legal complications, foreign exchange, hiring of ships, insurance, the problems of loading and unloading, commodity standards, and rules regarding payments. It was the meeting place of all races and creeds. Roman Catholics such as Laurensz. Spieghel and Cornelis Gijsbertsz. Plemp engaged in trade with Jews from Spain and Portugal. Merchants of various hues and tongues babbled over prices. The poet Jeremias de Decker saw the Exchange as a peace palace in which all peoples gathered in freedom and friendship. To him it was

A strolling place where Moor with Northman bargained
A church where Jew and Turk and Christian gathered
A school of every tongue, a market field of every ware
An exchange which swells all exchanges in the world.

To Vondel it

> *Received the burghers' life breath*
> *From old and new side of the town*
> *All foreign blood that afternoons collected here*
> *Flowed in a single auricle*
> *Fed by many veins*
> *Giving life to the body of the city.*

The fishing and cargo fleets originally came up to the Dam, now the Central Railroad station. From the early times there had been a weigh house there. In the sixteenth century a new harbor had been constructed, named the Rak, which means the division of a river into two roads. Not far distant was the *Schreirstoren* (weeping tower) from which sorrowful women watched their men go down to the sea in ships, many never to return. It was from hence that Henry Hudson set sail for what was to become New Amsterdam.

If one could not bring back the men and the ships lost to wave and gunshot, one could insure against losses. The

idea of insurance came slowly to Amsterdam. As late as
1564 the city looked upon insurance with suspicion. There
was, however, considerable private insurance, and on January 31, 1598, the city set up under government control
a chamber of insurance. It registered policies and intervened in claims and litigations. Soon it gained the confidence of the business community. By the close of the
seventeenth century, reinsurance was established in Amsterdam.

All Dutch port cities engaged in fishing, and Amsterdam was no exception. Travel descriptions mention constantly that the quays were filled with herring busses and
whaleboats, easily discernible even to the blind. Much of
the packing of herring for export was done over the
Sparendammerburg, and the largest fish market in the
world was on the Dam. Dutch fisheries first surpassed
those connected with the Hanseatic League, and throughout the seventeenth century conflicted with the English
fishermen, who resented and were jealous of the greater
Dutch success in their own occupation. One reason for
Dutch predominance in the fisheries was that government
controlled the methods of catching, curing, and marketing the fish. Dutch seafood then was better in quality, and
could usually be bought more cheaply than fish from any
other country. The Dutch also paid cash for the catch,
and many an Englishman homeward bound even from
Newfoundland sold his haul to a Dutch ship for a larger
and surer sum than he could realize in his home port.

Especially galling to the British were Dutch fish boats
off the English coast. Many acts were passed by Parliament
and the Privy Council to foster English fishing and to
exclude the Dutch from English waters. Attempts to ac-

complish the latter led Grotius to write the *Mare Liberum,* a legal treatise defending freedom of the seas. This was quickly answered by *Mare Clausum,* a work by the English legalist John Selden. English parliaments might pass acts and English writers like Sir Walter Raleigh and Josiah Child might complain about Dutch competition, but to no avail. The Dutch methods, especially their use of salt, were superior. Also Dutch mariners and fisherfolk worked harder. As the poet Andrew Marvell remarked:

> *How could the Dutch but be converted, when*
> *The Apostles were so many fishermen?*

As significant to Amsterdam as the fisheries was the grain trade, which helped feed Europe and made Amsterdam the granary of the continent. Amsterdam merchantmen carried wheat and other cereals to almost all European ports and returned with other items of trade destined for reshipment. So lively was the business that a special grain exchange (*korenbeurs*) became necessary. It was built in 1617 on the Oudenbrug. It consisted of an open space surrounded by a gallery supported by fifty-two columns. Under the wooden gallery each trader had a stall where he might display his wares. According to a foreign visitor: "Here is the great and general Store-House for Corn, of which tho' they have but little grown in their own Country, yet they serve their Neighbors with it and are great Dealers, some of their Merchants trading only in this Commodity are said to be worth above a hundred thousand Pounds Sterling."

The grain and fishery trades were closely intertwined with the Baltic. Although not so glamorous as the traffic with the Indies, the Baltic trade provided the foundation to Dutch economic activities throughout other parts of the world. The Dutch who superseded the Hanseatic League sent their ships farther up into the Baltic than did the English. Eventually the important grain, hemp, and flax ports at Danzig, Königsberg, and Riga became more and more dependent upon the Dutch middleman, who even froze British rivals out of the Russia trade via Archangel. Between 1610 and 1620, over two thousand ships paid tolls at the Danish Sound. Dutch ships averaged between sixty and seventy per cent of this number. Eighty per cent of all Baltic trade going through the Sound was in Dutch hands. Amsterdam was the leading Dutch city in this trade. Because of the shaky financial structures found in Baltic countries, bills drawn on Amsterdam and Hamburg were in the seventeenth century the customary means of payment used in the commercial centers of northern and central Europe. These two cities were hubs for the exchange of Baltic provinces. The English shippers presented a challenge to the Dutch only at Narva, Gothenburg, and Stockholm. Outside of the Baltic, Dutch factors sent yearly three hundred ships to Norway and brought home about 125,000 lasts of wood. About one-fourth of this unloaded at Amsterdam to be shipped to France predominately and to other European countries. Amsterdam's location on the North Sea, its great harbor and warehouse space, and the Dutch willingness to split their cargoes at many ports of call made Amsterdam the European emporium for Baltic products.

So great was Amsterdam's ascendency in the grain trade —a Bicker enterprise—that any scarcity in the larger areas of Europe was reflected on the Amsterdam grain exchange. In such times the Amsterdam grain merchants prospered.

The city's custom of storing large quantities of cereals against periods of want allowed Amsterdam merchants to realize lucrative profits from the misfortunes of others. They pushed up both the price of grain and freight rates, and the entire trade of the city was stimulated. Bountiful harvests in Europe had the opposite effect, but the merchants would buy great quantities cheap and wait for that rainy day. As late as 1666 three-fourths of the capital active in Amsterdam was estimated to be engaged in Baltic trade. In addition to the Bickers, other members of the *Vroedschap* accumulated fortunes in grain, shipping, shipbuilding, naval stores, and other commercial activities connected with northern Europe.

Another important business in the Baltic was the supplying of munitions to warring countries. Three merchants—Elias Trip, Stevan Gerard, and Louis de Geer—began to specialize in the munitions trade and about 1615 set up their business headquarters in Amsterdam. Four years later De Geer along with Willem de Besche began to develop Swedish iron and copper mines. By recruiting skilled metal-workers and gun-founders, De Geer in the second quarter of the century raised Sweden to first rank in munitions production. His brother Matthais and later his nephews, Jacob, Louis, and Hendrick Trip, became owners or lessees of extensive Swedish mining properties at a time when Swedish ore was the best in the world. Great Britain, for example, was eighty per cent dependent upon Swedish iron until the middle of the eighteenth century. De Geer's rival Trip had practically a monopoly on the export of Swedish copper and ran an extensive arms trade from Amsterdam.

During the Thirty Years' war, De Geer's warehouses

supplied not only the armies of Gustavus Adolphus and the States General but also those of Denmark, France, and the auxiliary troops of Ernest Count Mansfeld, Christian of Brunswick, and John of Saxe-Weimar. Between 1624 and 1648 De Geer claimed to have delivered 736,080 rix-dollars worth of war materials to the Swedish army. His estimated profits averaged about forty per cent a year. Throughout the seventeenth century Amsterdam remained the European market for war matériel. At the close of the century a contemporary said: "England and divers other Nations send to Amsterdam to buy Arms, Buff-Coats, Belts, Match, &. Yea, here are several Shopkeepers who can deliver Arms for four or five Thousand men and at a Cheaper rate than can be got any where else." As late as 1743 another contemporary remarked: "The Dutch are the most expert Founders in the World, and furnish most Countries with Ordinance. The German, Spanish, Italian, African, and Turkish have their Arms principally from Amsterdam; as their Cannon, Mortars, Powder, and Lead." Even Louis XIV was forced to "the Metropolis of an Enemy for Arms and Ammunition for his Troops." The indispensible ore that made these operations possible came from Sweden.

The Baltic was not the only inland sea where one could spot the Amsterdam flag. In 1590 the first Holland merchantmen ventured to pass through the Straits of Gibralter into the Mediterranean. This marked the beginning of a new trade, which was extremely detrimental to the Spanish, Portuguese, and Italian trading towns. The new operation was a hazardous one in the beginning because of Spanish warships and those of Barbary pirates. In 1611 the States General named Cornelis Haga the first Dutch diplomatic agent to the Sublime Porte. Shortly thereafter Amsterdam set up a commission to regulate trade to the Levant and to maintain a balance in the city's trade to the north and to the south of Europe. Jewish refugees from Spain, Portugal, and the Mediterranean cities probably gave advice on the Levant trade, but for the most part they did not have sufficient funds to be really active in such a long-range operation. Amsterdam goods and Dutch dollars were welcome in the Levant, and soon the Dutch began to dominate trade there.

Because of the wars with Spain and later with Portugal, Hollanders and Zeelanders were barred from trading with Spanish and Portuguese colonies. Not able to get what they wanted from the mother countries, the Dutch went to the sources of supply: spices from the East Indies, gold and ivory from Guinea, sugar from St. Thomas, salt from the Cape Verde islands, and wood and dyes from Latin America. Shortly after 1600 Amsterdam was taking more than a million guilders a year in high-priced articles from former Portuguese possessions. They included gold, ivory, pepper, skins, slaves, and sugar. For those commodities they traded textile and metal wares.

The most lucrative trade was with the Indies. One of the early problems facing the Dutch was how to get there. Petrius Plancius, that fiery Calvinist divine in Amsterdam's fight with Oldenbarevelt, was an early promoter of overseas explorations. An able geographer and astronomer, he sponsored, among other voyages, one searching for a northeast route to the Indies. Two ships were designated by the States of Holland to that purpose and Amsterdam contributed a third vessel. In July, 1594, the little fleet under Willem Barents (d. 1597) found open water, but was forced to turn back because it ran out of supplies. The next year the States General sent out seven ships only to have the mission frustrated by storms and icebergs.

The next venture was one of the most colorful in the history of voyages. In May, 1596, the Amsterdam government under proddings from Plancius sent ships out under the commands of Jacob van Heemskerck and Jan Cornelisz. de Rijp. The States General promised 25,000 guilders if they could find a successful passage north of Russia. De Rijp was forced back, but Heemskerck, guided by Barents, sailed on until his ship became frozen in the ice. He and his crew were forced to winter in Nova Zembla. The suffering was unbelievable. Barents and many of the crew ended up in icy Arctic graves, but Heemskerck and a portion of the crew managed late in 1597 to return home. The hair-raising descriptions of the expedition, especially the terrible winter, caused explorations for a northeast passage to be dropped. The expedition, however, contributed to the geographers' knowledge of Nova Zembla and Spitzbergen and was the talk of Europe. When Shakespeare has Fabian say to Sir Andrew, "You are now sailed into the North of my lady's opinion, where you will hang like an icicle on a Dutchman's beard," his audience could appreciate the reference. Truly the saga of Nova Zembla is one of the most exciting stories of Amsterdam history.

While Barents and his crew were sacrificing their lives for profit and knowledge, Amsterdamers were planning a new way to the Indies should the northeast route prove unfeasible. Cornelis Houtman of Gouda and Jan van Linschoten of Haarlem were drumming up interest in an approach via the Cape of Good Hope. Both men were knowledgeable about the Portuguese routes to India, especially Linschoten, who for a time had been a clerk to the Archbishop of Goa. His accounts of his voyage to India and his stay there and in places along the African Coast were highly instrumental in the decision of a group of Amsterdam merchants to send a fleet to India.

A "Compagnie van Verre" was organized by such men as Reynier Pauw, Peter Hasselaer, and seven other Amsterdam merchants. They, along with certain "participants," received permission from the States General to equip a fleet of four ships, carrying a total of 250 men, for the voyage to India. The squadron set sail on April 2, 1595, under Houtman's command. The ships reached Madagascar without much trouble, but storms and sickness detained them there for five months. From that island they sailed directly for Java and on July 22, 1596, arrived off Bantam. Because Portuguese traders had filled the natives with so many stories about the Dutch, Houtman was taken prisoner and released only on payment of a heavy ransom. He was forced to turn his course toward Molucca. When he reached Lombok, he had to abandon one of his ships. By that time his force had been reduced by disease to ninety men. On the homeward passage, Houtman went far to the south of Java and reached home on August 14, 1597. Church and tower bells pealed jubilantly as his ship triumphantly moored in the harbor. The city rejoiced. Houtman and his gallant crew were home safe—at least what was left of them. Wives and children might weep for those who did not return, but they were pretty much ignored. After all Houtman had in the hold of his ship 254 sacks of pepper, 25 lasts of nuts, and 30 bales of mace. The "Compaignie van Verre" made a profit of 27,000 guilders, adequate though not what it had hoped. Amsterdam had unlocked the door to the Indies.

The Dutch streamed through that door as East India companies were organized in Holland and Zeeland. A second company was founded in Amsterdam, and the two companies underwrote a new expedition to consist of nine ships under the command of Jacob van Neck and Wybrand van Waerwyck. It sailed in 1598 and also was successful. The ships were gone just fifteen months. To be sure two had been lost en route, but in the eyes of the Amsterdam Regents such a small price for such large profits was well worth the sacrifice. The riches of the Far East would henceforth come to Amsterdam to be reshipped all over Europe. Only the new Dutch companies posed a threat to Amsterdam's position.

The smaller companies in the East Indian trade were often hit heavily financially as they tried to establish themselves. Furthermore the competition between the companies was harmful to the interests of the nation as a whole. Oldenbarnevelt therefore had merchants most concerned meet with the States General and asked for a single unified company. After much discussion the United East India Company (VOC) was born on March 20, 1602.

Its charter shows the economic strength of Amsterdam as compared to the other cities concerned. Amsterdam contributed half of the capital of 6,500,000 guilders, which was raised by national subscription. It held twenty of the sixty seats in the general directory of the Company and had an even greater advantage in the general administrative directory. This group numbered sixteen working members. Representation was based on the proportion that each chamber in the country contributed to the original stock issue. Amsterdam had eight of the sixteen seats, Zeeland had four, while the other four seats were distributed among the other chambers according to the number of 300-guilder shares they had purchased. One additional member was nominated by the States General. The entire body is usually referred to in the literature as the Heeren XVII. Meetings were held for the first six years at Amsterdam, then two at Zeeland, then the rotation was continued. As the century progressed, Amsterdam with its ready capital bought more shares in the Company until the East India Company and Amsterdam became almost synonymous. It was at Amsterdam that the Company had its offices, its shipyards, its arsenal, its docks, and its warehouses.

The Heeren XVII were extremely powerful men, for the Company had almost sovereign rights. Acting in the name of the States General, it could make treaties with princes and other potentates, build forts, appoint governors and judicial officials in the territories under its control, and make privateering attacks upon Dutch enemies. It had a share in the spoils of all treasure ships that it might capture. Taxes on spices, silks, and cottons were not to be raised, but returning commanders of the fleets and the squadrons had to make a report to the States General. The Company paid the States General £5,000 yearly for its charter, but these sums were invested in the Company. Dividends varied, but the highest paid in a single year was fifty per cent. Of these Amsterdam received the lion's share along with the charges for building and outfitting the ships. These ships designed especially for the trade—called East Indiamen—for the most part unloaded their precious wares at Amsterdam's wharves and quays to be stored and sold at the best possible prices. Many an Amsterdam warehouse replaced the odors of fish and grain with the more pleasant scent of spices. The Company's most profitable year was perhaps 1669, when the Company owned 150 trading ships and 40 warships and employed ten thousand soldiers. Dividends for that year were forty per cent.

Another Dutch venture for trading overseas was the West India Company. Its role in the fall of Oldenbarnevelt has already been discussed. It will be remembered that it was primarily a privateering venture and Oldenbarnevelt's truce delayed its formation. Two months after the truce expired, the Company received its charter (June, 1621). It was open season on the Spanish colonies. There were five chambers or boards in the Company, each of which controlled a fixed portion of the joint capital. Amsterdam had nine-tenths of the total amount. Each chamber was to have a constant number of representatives in the general directory. Amsterdam had twenty while the others had only twelve or fourteen. The central administrative group consisted of eighteen directors from the chambers and one appointed by the States General. Together they made up the Heeren XIX. Amsterdam had eight in this body, Zeeland four, and the others two. The Heeren XIX were to meet for six successive years in Amsterdam, then one in Middleburg, and then the same rotation would continue. To the initial capital fund Amsterdam supplied nearly three of the seven million guilders.

Shortly after the Company was founded, the Regents of Amsterdam noted with considerable self-satisfaction that the Company was to all intents and purposes an Amsterdam venture. The Amsterdam chamber of the Company was dominated by South Netherlanders and Contra-Re-monstrants. For that reason there was less religious tolera-tion in New Amsterdam than in the mother city. After the Bicker League came into office, pressure was put on the Company to place more native Hollanders in positions of authority. Cornelis Bicker had been a director of the Com-pany from its beginning, but resigned shortly after Piet Heyn captured the Spanish silver fleet. He and his friends felt that Amsterdam's future lay in free trade with the new-ly conquered Brazil and with other Spanish possessions. As usual the city had its way. In 1639 considerable freedom was given to non-Company merchants trading with Brazil. Amsterdam refused to subsidize the Company unless the other chambers would carry their share of the load. The Company slid deeper and deeper into debt. To Amsterdam the Brazil venture had become a flop, and it had no desire to throw good money after bad. Consequently Brazil was lost to the Netherlands.

By 1649, Burgomaster Bicker regarded the West India Company as a lost cause and refused to spend Amsterdam money to line the pockets of Brabanters and Walloons. In 1674 the Company was forced into liquidation. A new company was formed the same year, but it never played a significant role in Dutch history. Professor Charles Box-er, one of the great authorities on the Dutch in Brazil and elsewhere during the seventeenth century, points out that the history of the Dutch West India Company cannot be understood without a knowledge of Amsterdam. It was the *de facto* capital of the Netherlands, and as so often in Netherland's history it was Amsterdam who "paid the piper and called the tune."

Willem Usselincx became dissilusioned with the monopolistic practices of the Dutch West India Company, withdrew from it, and went to Sweden where he received a charter for the *Söderkompanie*. His idealism was not sufficient to get the company started. It remained for two practical Amsterdamers, Samuel Blommaert and Peter Minuit, to move the venture from a dream to a reality. Blommaert was a merchant with interests in Sweden. Minuit had been a resident of Amsterdam for a long time and had served the West India Company as governor of New Amsterdam. When he went over to the new venture he brought other Company officials with him into the Swedish undertaking. The initial capital required to launch New Sweden was 48,000 guilders. Amsterdam supplied half of it.

When the first joint stock of the English East India Company went up for sale in 1614, the Amsterdamer Pieter Hoote came "knocking on the door." As a member of the Dutch East India Company, Hoote had lived thirteen years in the Indies. He now agreed to invest £4,000 in the English Company plus an additional £400 "for his freedom and the broke."

Foreigners envied Amsterdam with its warehouses bulging with every type of commodity imaginable. Amsterdam not only extended credits and stockpiled in the most important trades, it did the same for the lesser ones. The city streets were filled with the sights and smells of both exotic and nonexotic products. Across the quays one could view and smell the spices of the East, the fish and whale cargoes from many seas, sugar refineries processing sugar from the English and French West Indies, tobacco from Maryland

and Virginia destined for the Baltic and the European hinterlands, pitch and tar and the clean fresh odor of new woods—especially pine masts—from the Baltic.

The vast warehouses of Amsterdam formed a part of its architectural pattern and the life of its economy. Along with shipping, they made it possible for the Dutch to buy cheap and to hold for a sellers' market. Low interest rates, ample credit to merchants and artisans large or small, and government control of marketing gave Amsterdam its superiority over foreign trade rivals. Forests were purchased in Baltic countries even before they were cut as were the grape harvests in France before they were made into wine. Amsterdam merchants actually ran the wine trade in the Loire area. Through such tactics the Amsterdam merchant controlled the market. He withheld goods to raise prices. By dumping in times of plenty he could and sometimes did ruin foreign competition to such an extent that foreign merchants often became little more than Amsterdam factors. To carry out such policies it was necessary to tie up huge sums of capital in the warehouses.

Arent ten Grootenhuys owned four warehouses in the city, probably worth more than their assessed value of 15,000 guilders. Louis Trip's warehouses were valued at 9,910 guilders. Near the Texel quay were the munitions storehouses and close by were cellars in which brandy and tobacco were stored and which rented at 1,400 to 1,500 guilders. Along the Brouwersgracht were warehouses four to five stories high bulging with beer and strongly reinforced to prevent collapse under the excessive weight. It was out of this tradition that the world renowned Amstel and Heineken breweries evolved. The Herring-packers were near the Haarlem locks, and luxury items of every sort imaginable, along with books, could be found on the Warmussgasse. On the Osterburg were the East India Company storehouses, and the products of the whale fisheries were stockpiled in the "Greenland" storehouses. Dutch sugar-bakers could pay higher prices for raw sugar than could their English rivals because they built up reserves against periods of shortages. Stockpiling and better processing methods made it possible for Amsterdamers to undersell the British on the world market. By using the same methods Flemish sugar-bakers in London were driving the local sugar manufacturers to the wall. In 1640 an Amsterdam house purchased such large quantities of Russian furs that they forestalled the annual mart at Archangel to such an extent that when the fair opened there were hardly any furs to be had.

The stocking-merchant poet Vondel in *Zeemagazijn* and the locksmith-poet, Jan Hermansz. Krul, in *'T Palleys Der Amstelgoeden* (1636) left poems extolling and listing the riches of the Amsterdam warehouses and the broad variety of the commodities stored therein. There were items enough for any poet to handle. The price courant of 1635 showed 360 separate kinds of merchandise on sale in Amsterdam. By 1686 new trades and new items of different sorts raised the number to 505. Figures for the volume of trade in each category are difficult to come by, but the relative ebb and flow of the city's trade can be traced through the license and convoy fees paid into the Admiralty of Amsterdam. Because Amsterdam paid nine-tenths of the fees it is possible to trace the general value of the city's trade through years of plenty and years of war and disaster. The fees in 1589 were slightly over 237,746 guilders. They were over one half million guilders by 1611 and in 1636 went over the million mark. The increase fluctuated rather than progressed gradually. For example between 1651 and 1660 the receipts of the Admiralty did not total one million. In 1681 that mark was reached for the first time since 1668. The figure in 1699 was just a few thousand guilders shy of two million.

Amsterdam teemed with activity from within, for only a part of its citizens were engaged in foreign and overseas trade. Shipbuilding and the outfitting of ships were just a few occupations out of hundreds engaged in making products for foreign and domestic consumption. One English visitor made a tour of the city's many small markets concerned usually with the sale of a single product. There were a butter market, a cheese market, a poultry market, a spice market, a flower market selling cut flowers and potted plants, a dog market, a rag market, a tobacco market which sold pipes and tobacco boxes, a basket market, a chair market, a tub market, a pail market "all very pretty," a grain market, a biscuit market, a cake market, and an ale market. The Amsterdamers' love of dogs, tobacco, and flowers goes back a long way. The dog market was held every Monday morning, and an English traveler noted that about twenty "curs," all extremely ugly, were on sale that day. The women at that time like their modern sisters had to have a "hairy companion" and were willing to pay a good price for one. The Amsterdamer then could purchase almost anything on the open market. This is true even today on the open market held weekly on the Waterloo Plein. Today there are many flower markets, and small streets such as Albertcuypstraat fill up with stalls from which everything from herring to clothing can be obtained.

Amsterdam had two large butcher halls (*vlesshaals*), and the price of meat would have been more reasonable had it not been for a high excise tax. In addition each Jewish community had its own butcher shop. The stalls in the *vleeshaals* were well stocked, and the butchers and their wives were dressed much more cleanly than their counterparts in England. There was also a "Sawcidge, Hogsface and Tripe Market." The Bolonga "Sawcidges and dried Salmon" offered for sale were extremely tasty, "both of which they dress well, boiling in part, then frying . . . and eating it with Spinage, over which they scrape Nutmeg."

The city was filled with local industries and crafts. With the exception of the old cloth industry, most of these were continuations of the small businesses (*kleinbedrij*) of the Middle Ages. The new capitalism helped these small enterprises, but did not change them to the same extent as had been true in the larger trades. As one might expect, household industries in the main stayed fairly traditional with the business going from father to son as in the case of Vondel. A number of undertakings had a real division of labor, but of course without mechanization. Amsterdam craftsmen like those of the Middle Ages were independent, and their outlet was the city market places (*plaatselijke*). Usually the craftsmen were organized into guilds, which continued to play a role in Amsterdam's commercial life until well after 1672.

To obtain some idea of the prevalence of the guilds it might not be amiss to estimate the number of guilds, their membership, and their importance in the economic life of the city. Children born outside the city but of burgher parents, on reaching adulthood had to purchase burgher rights (*poorterschap*) to become members. They could avoid this edict by marrying the daughter of a burgher. The cost of burgher right was nominal, and the income was divided between the city and the city's orphanage (*burgherweeshuis*). In the middle of the seventeenth century the price was raised to fifty guilders. The advanced fee was detrimental to the craftsmen and to Amsterdam's retail trade. Consequently in 1668 the fee was lowered to twenty-eight stuivers. The laws dealing with burgher rights were cumbersome. Many nonnatives violated the restrictions and joined a guild before becoming freemen of the city. The *burgherweeshuis* officials who lost revenues when the laws were not enforced continually asked that the laws be carried out to the limit.

As a result of the *burgherweehuis* protests, the guilds in 1688 had to list their members and indicate who were natives and who were not. Thirty-seven guilds compiled and the lists were turned over to the orphanage. They appeared just at a time when Amsterdam's trade was to embark upon a new development which was to continue into the eighteenth century. The lists do tell us something about the guilds.

The largest guild was that of the tailors, with 881 members. This figure is interesting because the trend of the times was toward the industrial development of the cloth trade, and because Leiden was already outstripping Amsterdam in the making of textiles. Included in the tailors' guild were merchants who sold new and second-hand clothing. There were 36 in the furriers guild. The shoemakers and the tanners (*huidenkoopers*) numbered 343; in addition there were 658 cobblers including 94 who made wooden shoes (*klompenmakers*). This proportion would indicate that the majority of Amsterdamers by 1688 had abandoned wooden for leather shoes. There were 521 hatters, but this may be higher than the number earlier in the century because in 1687 a law had been passed allowing the hatters to employ as many helpers as they wanted. Although previously each shop could employ only eight workmen, one master and two good helpers could turn out 42 felt hats a day. There were 164 people in the cloth preparation guild (*lakenbereidersgildebroeders*), and the ribbon- and lace-makers guild which had been established as late as 1645 had 645 members.

After the clothiers next in sheer numbers were the builders and woodworkers. The house carpenters along with the furniture makers had a membership of 600 while the plasterers (*metselaars*) and the stone masons—who also worked in wood—consisted of 165 members. There were 400 master ship carpenters, and the coopers and wine cask makers who had their own guild distinct from the wood workers had 362 members, 45 of them basket weavers. The house painters and glass makers along with the artists were in the St. Lucas Guild. About ten per cent of the membership were artists, carvers, and sculptors. Within the guilds there were many divisions. The carpenters guild included furniture makers, chair makers, woodworkers, manufacturers of stocks for muskets and pistols, chest makers, manufacturers of the wooden gears found in looms, planers of wood, yardstick makers and workers in ebony.

The metal workers, numbering 238, were divided into seven specialties. There were 334 gold and silversmiths and 87 tinsmiths. The latter group admitted spoon makers. The number of tinkers listed is small, but there were 604 makers of glass, pottery, and tankards. Although

Amsterdam never became as well known in the manufacturing of pottery and porcelain as Delft, the Amsterdamers made and used more of the cheaper varieties and was Delft's best outlet. Pottery was replacing tin dishes on Amsterdam tables. There were all sorts of varieties of smiths then, and their seven crafts can be found in the old combined emblem of the St. Eloyengilde. Among the assortment of smiths both great and small could be found locksmiths, coppersmiths, cutlers, ship chandlers, and sword makers.

There were a sizeable number of occupations outside the guilds. Perhaps the best known are the diamond cutters and setters, who represented a new trade; when they began operations in 1600, there was no guild with which they could affiliate. Other occupations which do not appear on the guild registers thrived as the names of many Amsterdam streets mutely testify. The mighty *Heeren*, artists, ministers, and scholars have streets and parks named after them. The lesser folk are commemorated by the names of the narrow passages between the streets and the canals where they set up their shops or stalls, or perhaps by some preserved sign or gable stone. It is by their trades that the small streets and alleys of Amsterdam remembered the craftsmen of earlier days. In modern Amsterdam there is a shoe-lace makers street (Vetermakersgang), a pencil-makers street (Penseelmakersgang), a thread-makers street (Rijglifmakersgang), a skull-cap makers lane (Oorijsermakersgang), a shuttle-makers lane (Schietspoelmakersgang), a razor-makers lane (Scheerenmakersgang), a sieve-makers lane (Zeeftenmakersgang), a drum-makers lane (Trommelmakersgang), a cork-cutters lane (Kurksnijdersgang), a crocheters lane (Hakenmakersgang), a combmakers lane (Kammenmakersgang), a clasp-makers lane (Krammenmakersgang), and a diamond street (Diamantsstraat). The list could undoubtedly be expanded by scholars such as Mr. Simon Hart of the Amsterdam city archives.

The majority of the businesses in Amsterdam were small ones employing six to ten people in a single shop. However, there were some large establishments. When the Bleau printing establishment went up in flames in 1672 the damage was estimated at 335,000 guilders. This was only one of the Bleau plants. In 1660 when the sugar refinery of Van Nuyts on the Herengracht facing the Warmoesgracht suffered a similar fate, the loss was set at 300,000 guilders. These were the exceptions. It was only after the influx of French Huguenots into Amsterdam after 1680 that the larger industries became more common. Also it was only after 1672 that Amsterdam became a city of millionaires. In 1624 the richest man in Amsterdam left an estate of 920,000 guilders. His fortune came not from industry but from land speculation in the Beemster and from overseas trade.

Sometimes small operations mushroomed into large enterprises. Textile processing, beer manufacturing, sugar refining, tobacco curing, soap making, and the printing and selling of books have to be considered big businesses by seventeenth-century standards. None of these better known industries was organized into a guild except the printers and booksellers, whose membership totaled 186. The others were organized a little differently. They had their own college of overseers such as the beer college, the soap-boilers' college, and the college formed for the sugar refiners. These groups regulated their members along guild lines. Furthermore, city officials inspected the seal on all manufactured goods to see if they measured up to prescribed standards.

Much of the making of textiles was done in the home, but there was a tendency for the larger operators to hire young girls and older women from the charitable institutions. These unfortunates lived at the charitable institutions and often worked for a pittance. English cloth makers obtained most of their "fraaie" colors from Amsterdam dyers, and prints of the city done by E. Stoopendaal and Balthazar Florisz. show textiles drying in racks located on the housetops of the dyers or spread out on fields just outside the city walls. The majority of textile works were located in 1625 on the Nieuwendijk between the Gravenstraat and the Kolkje. Woolens, linens, and the other cloths, lumped under the term "new draperies," were sent to England and elsewhere. Silk weaving did not achieve any real significance until the eighteenth century.

Many of the textile houses on the Nieuwendijk were eventually replaced by sugar refineries. In 1605 there were only three sugar refineries in this area. Fifty years later the number had climbed to sixty. Amsterdam by that time had become the greatest processor of sugar in the world. Dutch know-how in this occupation was excellent. Later when Dutch refugees applied the same techniques in London that they used at home, they forced London refiners out of business.

Amsterdam in the seventeenth century made great strides in tobacco processing, in brewing, and in distilling. These last two industries needed wooden casks as did the shippers. Consequently sawmills and other types of mills sprang up everywhere. Milling was so lucrative that they could be found in all sorts of places—on the bastions of the city walls, on land outside the walls, and along the quiet canals and *grachts*. The wood millers and the grain millers were combined in a single guild of 94 members. Rembrandt's father and brother were millers just outside Leiden.

Another vital industry was soap manufacturing. The number of persons engaged in that trade must have been considerable. Suffice to say that Amsterdam black soap was famous throughout the world. Glass works were important not only at home where they made the long thin glasses for Dutch cordials and gin, but also in the overseas trade because of the demand for glass trinkets by the natives of Africa and North America. A glass factory required considerable capital. Jan Jansz. Carel obtained it the hard way. He is an excellent example of a man advancing to a larger business from a smaller one. He began in the butter and cheese trade, but in 1601 he built a glass factory on the Kloveniersburgwal, which employed approximately eighty men. They produced drinking glasses, mirrors, and beads. Another glass works of reputation was built on the Muntplein by an Abraham van Tongerloo. This plant burned down in 1612 and was removed to the Keisergracht. When the Gereformeerd Gymnasium was built in 1930, the remains of Tongerloo's first factory were much in evidence.

Another thriving industry was the printing and selling of books. Although the press in Amsterdam was not without legal restrictions (*wettelijk*), it was virtually free in comparison with the presses in other European countries. Dutch and foreign books were printed in staggering numbers and the total publication of books and pamphlets ran into the thousands. In Amsterdam between 1660 and 1670, volumes were printed in Low German, Latin, French, English, Spanish, Welsh, medieval Latin, High German, Greek, Hebrew, Syrian, Bohemian, Danish and of course Dutch. An Armenian Bible was also printed in the city. The earliest English newspapers circulating in England came off Amsterdam presses. The number of printers are many, but the three most important houses were those of Jans., Bleau, and Elzevier.

The most significant commodity that Amsterdam handled was money. Permission to export monetary metals was rare in the seventeenth century. The Exchange Bank of Amsterdam, however, enjoyed a considerable amount of freedom which not only made profits for the bank but stabilized exchange rates in Amsterdam and elsewhere. This encouraged the circulation of bills of exchange as negotiable instruments of credit, and the discounting and sale of bills of credit became a lively business in the city. The importing and exporting of money became highly lucrative. The capture of the Spanish treasure fleet in 1628 may have helped Amsterdam become a center for bullion as did some of the loot from other Spanish vessels, but that was only part of the story. The firm confidence that European depositors had in the bank was also a vital factor in its success. Princes and prelates sent money to the Amsterdam bank to have it minted and exchanged for goods and services, or to buld up financial cushions should their military and political affairs come to ruin.

Many such accounts in the Exchange bank were substantial and often listed under fictitious names. For example we do not know how many English Commonwealth men were putting funds in the bank in 1652, or how much the Earls of Danby and Shrewsbury deposited in 1688. The Amsterdamers accepted bullion or money, but quite often showed their contempt for the customers and occasionally addressed them in sharp language. Amsterdam provided the best service and their blue-blooded clients had to take it. Sometimes, however, burgher arrogance misfired. One Amsterdam merchant while traveling in a country about whose prince he had made some derogatory remarks was arrested by the prince and then freed with the reminder: "Henceforth Commonwealth Man have a care how you treat Sovereign Princes, for the unmannerly Freedom you take at home, might cost you your life abroad."

The rise of the Amsterdam exchange was a slow one. Philip of Burgundy gave the city the right to set up a money exchange in 1440, and the new institution based its use of paper money on the Antwerp exchange. The Regents decided in 1606 to set up an exchange bank on the model of Seville or Venice. The Amsterdam venture was based mostly on the Venetian Banco de Rialto, although the Royal Exchange in London was also known to Amsterdam merchants. Whatever the main source, the Exchange Bank of Amsterdam began business in January, 1609.

The bank's function from the beginning was the acceptance of deposits, the transfer of accounts, the exchange of money, the purchase of precious metals and bullion, and other functions in the capitalistic tradition of seventeenth-century Amsterdam. Needless to say, space prohibits going into the detailed operations of the Amsterdam exchange. No one can write on the subject without a great debt to Professors J. G. van Dillen and Violet

Barbour. During the "Golden Age" the bank concerned itself mostly with exchange and deposit banking. Thus it was spared the risk of discounting notes and lending money to individuals. It did advance sums to the Lending Bank of Amsterdam, to the East India Company, and to Amsterdam itself. Throughout the seventeenth century its economic position was never precarious. The first run on the bank occurred in 1672, and the "institution was saved by high metallic coverage."

The bank's high standards helped make Amsterdam the center of European exchange. As a cashier it provided a secure and convenient system of exchange that was not rivaled elsewhere in Europe. Sir William Temple looked at the Dutch Exchange Bank as "the greatest Treasure either real or imaginary, that is known anywhere in the World. The place of it is a great Vault under the Staathouse, made strong with all the circumstances of Doors and Locks, and other appearing cautions of safety that can be." The Commissioners for the bank had a room in the City Hall, and the treasure of the bank was in the basement. The burgomaster was the only one with authority to inspect the vaults, so to the foreigner the wealth of the bank was an unknown quantity. Contemporaries undoubtedly exaggerated its wealth—and the Amsterdamers preferred it that way—but most foreigners knew it was a safe place for deposits and reliable in exchange. As Temple remarked, the credit of the bank was the credit of the city, "whose Stocks and Revenues is equal to that of some Kingdoms." Confidence in the bank along with its reserves made it the most singular financial institution in seventeenth-century Europe.

Government supervision and regulation aided the bank

and prevented it from many financial errors. The *Vroeds-chap* decreed that all monetary transactions of over 600 guilders had to clear through the Exchange Bank. This ordinance was a direct borrowing from Venetian banking. The bank assessed a three per cent penalty on overdrawn accounts and closed in the second half of January to close the books. February 2 was the starting date for each financial year. No Amsterdam merchant who accounted himself for anything failed to have an account at the bank, and its operation was world-wide.

The bank from the start had been charged with providing bullion for the mints. So well did it carry out that obligation, and so honestly did the mint strike its coins, that Amsterdam money was recognized as the soundest in Europe. Russia, for example, insisted that all countries except England, who paid in rubles, meet their financial obligations with Dutch currency.

The financial structure of the city attracted money to Amsterdam. England, laboring under mercantilistic legislation, was for all its laws bled white by the Amsterdam Exchange. Amsterdam contrary to seventeenth-century ideas permitted the export of monetary metals. In 1683 the mintmaster informed the States General that the normal annual importation of silver would be between 15,000,000 and 18,000,000 guilders. Of that amount 13,000,000 might leave the country. The monetary policies and the relatively free capitalism of Amsterdam brought people from distant lands and in various financial positions to the Amsterdam Beurs, whose open arcades accommodated all comers. In the rush hours between noon and one o'clock, Germans, Poles, Hungarians, Walloons, Frenchmen, Spaniards, Russian, Turks, and at times even

Hindus "shouldered one another in a polylingual hubbub of bargaining." Amsterdam's pre-eminence as a money market grew even stronger in the eighteenth century.

The investments of Amsterdamers in international trade have been hinted at above. Men such as Louis de Geer and Elias Trip along with others loaned Gustavus Adolphus of Sweden 250,000 guilders on the security of the Swedish copper mines. The Trip house on the Kloveniersburgwal and the De Geer home on the Herengracht testify to their success in this and other ventures. When Trip died in 1636 the Swedish crown owed him 864,000 guilders. The De Geer family was raised to the Swedish peerage. In nearly every European country, Amsterdam capitalists were active.

The Exchange was of course a center for speculation. The idea of dealing in futures—especially in the spice trade—was perhaps the brain child of a Portuguese Jew, Baron Suasso. It was said that on a single day he made 100,000 *écus* by knowing about the death of the king of Spain five or six hours before the Exchange. The number of negotiable stocks in the seventeenth century was rather small. The plungers were provided with an outlet by speculating on political events or on the shifting political scenes. If the unpredictability of politics was not sufficiently risky, the Amsterdamer could always gamble in the tulip mania.

Although it did not have the international reputation of the Exchange Bank, a second bank was established in 1614. This was the Loan Bank (*Bank van Leening*) which played a vital role in the city's economic life. About it the British economist Josiah Child said in 1688: "In Holland . . . any man that is a competent good Husband, Prudent and Careful in his business, may take up to £500 or £1,000 at 3 per cent. upon his own Note only, whereas in England where the present rate is double, the Usurers require three good Mens Bonds at the least for £500 at 6 per cent." The situation was not so ideal as the foreigners thought. Often Amsterdamers with established credit would borrow at a low rate of interest and then float loans at higher rates both in Holland and abroad.

The Loan Bank advanced capital to small businesses, but it appears that the charges varied with the solvency of the applicant. The bank began with a capital of 1,200,-000 guilders. In the next year it was doubled. Interest rates fluctuated between five and six and one-quarter per cent. The Loan Bank competed so successfully with the Lombard brokers that soon all that was left of the Italian bankers was their name on the street where once they had done their business. From the beginning the Loan Bank was a civic project. The Exchange Bank, the city treasury, and private citizens invested in it and helped it through its growing pains. In 1622 the Poor Relief Office (*Weeskammer*) began to invest its funds in the institution. The bank prospered. By 1685 it was able to liquidate its debts to the early subscribers and held a working capital of approximately a million guilders.

After 1621 private banks sprang up in the city. These had been outlawed shortly before the founding of the Exchange Bank, but it was not long before they were back in business. They were allowed to hold bills in current money, but not to the extent of the Exchange. The individual or private banking establishments were not so hampered by restrictions as were city institutions. The nonmunicipal banks were the forerunners of credit companies and installment buying. They prevented the Exchange Bank and the Loan Bank from becoming monopolies, but they were not so sound financially. In times of crises such as the continued warfare after 1672 many of them were ruined.

The booming commercial community of Amsterdam not only had capital for business and speculative ventures, but it had a social conscience as well. That conscience was not the same as that found in the Middle Ages or in a modern socialist state, but the wealthy burghers made substantial contributions to charity. Common laborers might be victimized by economic fluctuations and by exploitation, but they did have a higher standard of living than the rest of Europe. Furthermore there was money available to help the unfortunate. The burghers also invested money to foster the city's aesthetic, artistic and intellectual growth. Amsterdam was more than a market for the world. It filled its warehouses with material goods, but it had intellectual storehouses as well. There are few instances in modern history when the historical, the aesthetic, the social, the economic, and the metaphysical blended so completely as they did in seventeenth-century Amsterdam. The city knew how to make money, and the citizens knew how to spend it. Perhaps the airs of the Amsterdam burgher were open to ridicule by English, French, and Italian intellectuals. Yet cultural ideas in Amsterdam undoubtedly reached deeper socially than in London or Paris, or, for that matter, in any European city during the first three quarters of the seventeenth century.

CHAPTER FOUR

The Dissemination of Knowledge

DURING THE MIDDLE AGES, Amsterdam had hardly distinguished itself as a center of culture. As compared with the neighboring ecclesiastical see of Utrecht and with Antwerp at its height, Amsterdam had been intellectually barren. Yet it had not been completely devoid of things of the mind. The many religious houses had fostered education, and as early as 1342 the city had its own Latin school. At the time of the Alteratie there were two Latin schools, one in the Oude Kerk and the other on the Nieuwe Zijde. These schools were Calvinized, and throughout the great period of Amsterdam they played a useful role. In 1678 the two schools were united.

Amsterdam may not have contributed as much to learning as some other cities, but it did provide an intellectual climate for such men as Descartes, Locke, Le Clerc, and Spinoza, to mention a few. Like the goods on the market place, products of the mind were often imported and then shipped throughout Europe. The presses of Amsterdam worked mightily to spread new ideas. People ranging from Galileo and Descartes to Voltaire could have their books printed in Amsterdam at a time when their homelands banned them. It was in Amsterdam that Locke's *Essay on Toleration* was first printed, and the example of the city plus the urgings of his friends influenced his thinking.

Amsterdam was a burgher society. The salon of a merchant could hardly compare with those of kings and nobles. On the other hand, literature, art, and learning probably reached down to a larger segment of the population than they did in any other contemporary city. Admittedly much of the scholarly investigation was done by amateurs who devoted a large portion of their lives to trade, industry, or government, or perhaps to a combination of all three. A sizeable number of them, however, did have some kind of a degree, usually in theology or medicine. Who could deny that the stocking trader Vondel, the aristocrat and government official Pieter Hooft, the lens-grinder Spinoza, the bookkeeper Leeuwenhoek, the doctor Tulp, the printers Bleau, Hondius, and Lodewijk Elzevier, the many sided Manasseh ben Israël, and countless other nonacademics made real contributions to learning and to the spread of knowledge?

Seventeenth-century Amsterdam placed a heavy emphasis on education, which could be gained either in school or out. Foreigners continually pointed out that the Dutch youth of both sexes were better trained in language, speech, geometry, and arithmetic than were the children of any other European country. They were especially impressed with the education of young women, who, after marriage, were quite capable of carrying on their husbands' affairs should the occasion warrant it.

There were many opportunities in Amsterdam for a child to receive the rudiments of an education. Since there were probably no public schools as we understand them today, it was more difficult for the very poor to obtain instruction. The orphanages offered some formal academic courses along with religious instruction and the mastery of a trade—usually spinning and weaving. In the Deacons' Orphanage the very young during the summer attended classes eight hours a day. In winter the number of hours was reduced to six. As they grew older more time was spent teaching skills which might provide a livelihood. Both sexes attended classes, and the older children who might be farmed out during the day to work were provided with instruction in the evening. Twice a year the youths were examined for their progress in reading, writing, and religion. The orphanages of the Walloons, Collegiants, Mennonites, and English Presbyterians all provided the young with a knowledge of at least reading and writing. Furthermore it is probable that children of poor parents, were sent to the orphanages to be educated in the three R's and to learn a trade.

There were other roads to learning for those able to pay. A third Latin school was set up on the Oostzijd van de Singel between the Regulierstoren by the Kloosterstraat. It contained six grades and the student ordinarily remained in each class for half a year and was then promoted. By the time a student reached fifteen he supposedly was old enough to attend the university. The new university at Leiden required that all matriculants know Latin. Thus considerable effort was made in both the public and private schools to instruct prospective university students in that language. Because of the bilingual nature of the Low Countries, French was also in demand. So was mathematics.

Two Amsterdam schoolmasters made significant contributions to teaching. Jan van den Velde helped perfect Dutch calligraphy. He did a number of excellent copybooks, drawing his examples from baroque varieties of the virtuoso curlicues of his day. His books with writing samples were printed into Latin, Dutch, French, and English by Willem Jansz. Bleau and others. One of his best known works, his *Spieghel der Schrijfkonste* (*Mirror of Writing Art*), went through many editions and influenced handwriting both in Holland and abroad.

Another Amsterdam schoolmaster of renown was Willem Bartjens (c. 1593–1673). He opened a school in the Pijlsteeg near the Warmoesstraat in 1591 and wrote a ciphering book, *Cijferinghe* . . . (1633), which made his name immortal. From that work generations of Amsterdamers and others learned the mysteries of calculations, and the proverb "he can cipher like Bartjens" became the highest praise for proficiency in arithmetic. Vondel studied under Bartjens. He subsequently wrote a poem of dedication to one of the later editions of the *Cijferinghe* in which somewhat overenthusiastically he compared his old teacher to Euclid. Bartjens wrote other books on arithmetic and bookkeeping advertised to be "necessary for all merchants." His motto, "God is my salvation," indicates in part how closely trade, learning, and religion were intertwined.

Books of all sorts were readily available. They ranged in subject matter from calligraphy to cartography. Very popular were pattern books, readily available, and which gave instruction in everything from furniture making to the building trades. Amsterdam printers went in for volume sales and were not too concerned about the beauty of such books. Visual aids in the form of copious illustrations abounded in great variety. Books could be had on geography with highly illustrated atlases, on agriculture, the making of fortifications, and the building of ships. All were well illustrated with charts and diagrams. When Nicholas Witsen published his work on naval architecture (1671), Samuel Pepys, diarist and naval secretary, marveled that the Dutch had schools to teach shipbuilding and mechanics, and "that strangers may come and learn as well as natives." Shortly after Pepys's comment, Peter the Great of Russia came to Holland to study shipbuilding in a small town just outside Amsterdam.

Vondel's education is perhaps a good illustration of what could be achieved educationally by the nonacademic. He was a child of a lower middle-class family. A son of Anabaptist refugees, Vondel had been born in Germany after his parents fled from Antwerp. He was very young when he came to Amsterdam and evidently attended Bartjen's school and learned reading, writing, and arithmetic necessary to read the Bible and to carry on the stocking-making trade of his father. He picked up French either at home or from the Brabanters who lived in the neighborhood, but, unlike his better off contemporaries, he had no training as a youth in the classical tongues. He also differed from Shakespeare because later in life he was not content to know "little Latin and less Greek." While running an active business, Vondel by means of unwearying labor learned Latin from Hayo Gabbema to such a proficiency that he could write tragedies on the model of Seneca and satires in the style of Horace. Later in life he acquired a command of Greek and came to prefer Sophocles to the more bombastic Roman dramatists.

As a historian he was self-taught, but what a magnificent feat of pedagogy he achieved! His poetic epics, all factually sound, treat such diverse personages as the Emperor Constantine, Mary Stuart, and the Amsterdam hero Gijsbrecht van Amstel. His historical inspiration came from the life around him, and he loved to revel in the past of the city he adored. He knew Amsterdam's past and present better than any other of its citizens and was one of the best educated men of his time. For all his learning and understanding of the broad vistas of history ranging from the Roman Forum to the White Sea, no matter where his imagination carried him, Vondel was always an Amsterdamer. He found, however, intellectual contentment in the classics and in the baroque.

Pieter Hooft's educational Odyssey followed a different route. Cornelis, his father, was of merchant stock and was one of the most influential burgomasters of Amsterdam during the period following the Alteratie. Hooft's Baptist mother belonged to the Bleau family, illustrious in the annals of Dutch printing. Hooft was sent to the Amsterdam Latin School and at the young age of sixteen wrote a classical drama, *Archilles and Polyxena*. He was steeped in the classics, especially Ovid and Seneca. Hooft also had a command of French, Italian, and Spanish, which opened to him the doors of the Renaissance. He toured France, Italy, and Germany and enrolled at Leiden, where he studied under the great humanist scholar Daniel Heinsius (1580/1–1655). Hooft returned to Amsterdam in 1608, and the next year was made Drost of Muiden and Baljuw of Gooiland. He held this dual post—usually reserved for the nobility—for the rest of his life. At Muiden Castle, just outside of Amsterdam and where he resided for a good part of the year, Hooft surrounded himself with artists, authors, and musicians. This group was the renowned *Muiden Kring* (Muiden Circle), a salon of tremendous significance in the intellectual life of Amsterdam and Holland.

It was possible for the eager student by paying fees to obtain a good education in Amsterdam outside formal academic institutions. Amsterdam had all sorts of learned people who for a price were willing to share their knowledge with others. Doctors, apothecaries, lawyers, civil servants, book sellers and publishers, men of letters, artists, school masters, ciphering masters, navigators and others took in apprentices, gave lectures, wrote and sold books, and tutored to such an extent that Amsterdam soon rivaled the university town of Leiden as a center of Dutch learning.

Many refugees contributed to the city's intellectual life. How John Robinson taught at Leiden to raise funds for his band of pilgrims is an often told tale; there were people trading knowledge for bread within the walls of the city on the IJ who were even more learned than Robinson.

Henry Ainsworth came to Amsterdam from Swanton in Norwich, and at first was associated with the Reformed Church. He dwelled on the Singel by Hierpoort, and made significant contributions to scholarship in Hebrew. He at first was employed by a bookdealer for nine stuivers a week and was so poverty stricken that he was forced to "live on boiled roots." This Brownist leader from the University of Cambridge was a Hebrew scholar superior to anyone on the Leiden faculty. He may have been the best Hebraist in Europe. His commentaries on the Bible, in which he cites such Jerusalem authorities as Thargum,

Brershit Rabbah, Jarchi (Raschi), and Chizkoeni, were outstanding achievements in scholarship as was his introduction to the Pentateuch in which he used the Codex of Maimonides.

Another noteworthy English scholar was Matthew Slade, who was at first received with open arms by Ainsworth but within a year kicked out of the Brownist congregation. In 1598 he obtained a position at the Latin School in the Koelstraat, and four years later was appointed rector. Slade too was an excellent Hebraist and just missed obtaining a professorship in theology at the University of Franeker. He married the stepdaughter of Petrius Plancius, and began to make Arabic translations. That language had been dead in Europe since the seventh century. Slade became keeper of the Amsterdam Library, located at the time in the Nieuwe Kerk. Later he catalogued the library. Other learned Englishmen in Amsterdam were Hugh Broughton and John Paget. The former wrote a chronological history of the world, which linked the Bible with history, and the latter not only preached in the English Church and wrote polemics against the sects, but also supervised the church school.

As might be expected, the Jews of the Sephardim advanced Hebrew studies. Manasseh ben Israël made Amsterdam the center of the Hebrew book trade, which previously had been located in Venice. In 1645 Emanuel Benveniste, recently from that city, produced the famous uncensored Amsterdam edition of the *Talmoed*. Later in the century Joseph Athias was given a chair and a gold medal by the States General for his excellent Hebrew Bible. Many of the Hebrew contributions were closely linked with religion, but not all the Jewish community restricted its interest to theology. Joseph de la Vega wrote a remarkable book, *Confusion de Confusiones,* which exposed the many tricks used by stockholders to manipulate the market. The united *Talmoed Tora* was the basis for religious instruction of the Jewish lower classes and an inspiration for those intellectual Jews who helped make Amsterdam a significant center for Jewish learning. In medicine, Abraham Zucato and Ephriam Bueno (whose portrait Rembrandt painted) rendered a real service to medical knowledge, and they practiced with standards that compared favorably with any of their learned Gentile contemporaries.

Jan Theunisz.'s career was associated with both English and Jewish refugees. He was a friend to Slade and probably to Joseph Pardo. He was also acquainted with Broughton and the Jew, David Farar. Theunisz. was a Baptist and early in his life had been connected with printing in Leiden. In Amsterdam in 1605 he published the first book in Greek-letter type. He became an Arabic scholar, and after the death of Joseph Scaliger in 1609 the center of Arabic studies moved from Leiden to Amsterdam. Theunisz. probably learned Turkish from Joseph Pardo, but a Polish Jew had been teaching it in the city earlier. Theunisz. accepted a teaching post at the University of Leiden and left his wife in Amsterdam to run the family distillery. His experience as a faculty member was an unhappy one. He returned shortly to Amsterdam, where he wrote religious tracts and held a famous debate with Thomas Laemer over the meaning of the first words in the Bible. In 1617 he was appointed Professor of Hebrew at Samuel Coster's Academy.

That institution has a unique role in the history of

learning and literature in Amsterdam. Writers such as
Hooft and Bredero and other Amsterdam men of letters
were interested in the advancement of the Dutch language.
They objected to the excessive use of artificial Latin
phrases, and held the opinion that the Dutch language in
itself had value. This reaction was in part the result of
the Renaissance stress on the use of the vernacular, but it
is well to remember that the Dutch language had been
pretty much at the mercy of the intellectuals, writers, and
preachers. It had never had the support of a brilliant court
or of an aristocracy in the ordinary European sense. Furthermore the educational needs of Amsterdam's mercan-
tile society demanded something different from a curricu-
lum based on the classics. A more practical approach was
wanted. Thus it is highly understandable why a teacher
such as Willem Bartjens would back Coster's educational
views.

The Dutch Academy was launched in 1617. This new
educational institution was intended to be a "Netherlands training school." Influenced by the academies in
the Italian cities, Coster planned to give instruction in
the vernacular, a scheme completely at odds with the practice at Leiden. Courses were to include Hebrew, mathematics, history, and Greek philosophy. The school building, located on the west side of the Keizersgracht, included
a theater, which as time went on became more important
than the Academy itself. The Academy opened in Septem-
ber, 1617, with a play which showed the Muse of the Amsterdam burghers opening the doors of learning in both
science and the arts.

Coster, the force behind the school, hoped that in the
Academy "the sciences too would bring their industry to

bear, to edify the citizenry for love's sake and to enlighten it with the touch of the Dutch language." Hebrew and mathematics were taught to "an incredible multitude of people," and plans were in the air to convert the Academy into a national university. The times, however, were not propitious. A year after the founding of the Academy the Synod of Dort was convened, and to the Amsterdam Calvinists the ideas of the Academy appeared dangerous. The suspicions of the Academy's enemies were heightened by the fact that its first two instructors, Theunisz. and Sybrandt Hansz. Cardinael, were both Mennonites. Cardinael, a cartographer of no mean repute, had gained teaching experience in a school in the Nieuwe Nieuwestraat. He had published text books on the use of the Dutch language and in history, and was one of the best teachers of his day in astronomy, navigation, and mathematics. It is estimated that between 1617 and 1618 over two thousand persons profited from Cardinael's instruction.

While storm clouds gathered around him, Coster's hopes and imagination soared into unreality. He planned to offer instruction in astronomy, mathematics, medicine, law, etc. Needless to say the medical and legal colleges took a dim view of what they considered would be popular law and folk medicine. Pressure mounted. The instructional part of the Academy was closed by the burgomasters in 1623, but the theater continued to operate. Coster returned to the practice of medicine. Cardinael went back to the school on the Nieuwe Nieuwestraat. Theunisz. purchased a house, now 23 Oudebrugsteeg, which a year later he converted into a music hall named either *D'Os in de Bruyloft* or *'t Huys te Sinnelust*. Here concerts were given daily. The customers might try their hand with the house musical instruments or watch puppet shows while the host sold them liquid refreshments. Theunisz. had gone from lecturer at Leiden and professor at Amsterdam speaking on matters concerning the Spirit to Amsterdam publican hustling drinks. Yet in this music house the Swiss Eusebius Meisnerus gave lessons in Latin and Greek. It is also possible that the German Joannes Christenius, who founded a new Greek and Latin school in 1632, may at one time have given instruction in the *'t Huys te Sinnelust*. There, Apollo and Bacchus joined forces.

Although the Academy of Coster might be closed, the forces of liberalism in Amsterdam were not to abide forever the decrees of the Synod of Dort. The Remonstrants soon returned to Amsterdam. The town fathers were not blind to the city's need for higher education. On the last day of 1629 the *Vroedschap* decided that the city needed its own professor of philosophy. That decision supplied the motive for founding the *Athenaeum Illustre*. A year later, December 11, 1630, it was decided to appoint two professors to organize a *doorluchtig Gymnasium* (illustrious school or *Athenaeum Illustre*). Geradus Joannes Vossius and Caspar van Barlaeus were selected. There was a considerable difference between the Academy of Coster and the *Athenaeum Illustre*, but surely Coster and his friends helped pave the way for the latter.

The school encountered opposition from all sides. The University of Leiden was against the plan and suggested that Amsterdam found another Latin school connected with the University so that the better prepared students would matriculate there. Coster's old enemies, the Swiss Academy and the Reformed Church, took their usual obscurantist positions, and this time their chief complaint was that the two professors were Remonstrants. They took the matter to the States of Holland, which skillfully side-stepped the issue. The matter was then referred to the Council of the States General and to the Court of Holland, which on December 22, 1631, granted permission for the city to go ahead with its plans. Amsterdam would probably have gone its own way with or without approval, because as early as May, 1631, the *Heeren* had more or less installed the two professors and provided them with housing. Vossius was granted moving expenses and a salary of 2,500 guilders along with 900 more to meet living charges while Barlaeus received 1,500 and an additional 900 for expenses.

The reputation of Vossius, one of the best known scholars of his time, was based more on his ideas about antiquity than his thoughts on predestination. He held an honorary degree from Oxford and at one time had been offered a professorship in history at Cambridge. Barlaeus, somewhat overshadowed by Vossius, was well known in the fields of theology and philosophy and at one time had practiced medicine. On January 8, 1632, Vossius gave his inaugural address entitled *"Het Nut der Geschiedenis"* ("The Use of History"). The next day Barlaeus lectured on *"Mercator Sapiens."* The Regents struck a silver penny to commemorate the opening, and Hooft and Vondel celebrated the occasion with verse. Thus began the long and indeed "illustrious" history of an institution which in 1876 officially became the University of Amsterdam. Courses in medicine and theology were added in the seventeenth century along with law, Greek, oratory, and Oriental languages. In this last field Holland was the nursery for Western Europe.

Of importance to subsequent scholars, the burgomasters had the library in the Nieuwe Kerk moved to the top floor of the Athenaeum. This collection catalogued by Slade became the nucleus of the University of Amsterdam libraries. Soon, in addition to a fine manuscript collection, it included books on almost every subject and in all of the tongues known to scholarship. In the seventeenth century it was open Wednesdays and Saturdays from two to five. Once more the *Vroedschap* had made learning and the tools of scholarship the property of the city rather than of the Reformed Church. To this day, the University of Amsterdam, unlike other Dutch universities, is a municipal foundation.

The guilds gave instructions in their arts and trades and saw to it that members maintained high standards of proficiency. The College of Medicine inspected and examined midwives and apothecaries and maintained a *Hortus Medicus*. Here all the known plants were gathered, and to the *Hortus Medicus* the apprentices of apothecaries came to be tested in their knowledge of herbs, a field so vital in seventeenth-century medicine. Amsterdam printers published herbals, and by the seventeenth century, Amsterdam replaced Venice and Lisbon as the world's center in the drug trade.

There was also a College of Surgeons in Amsterdam, which had rooms over St. Anthonie's Weigh House. Here, as the canvasses of Amsterdam artists illustrate, anatomy lessons were given in Dutch twice a week to surgeons and their apprentices. The most famous of these is undoubtedly "The Anatomy Lesson of Dr. Tulp." Rembrandt later in life showed Tulp's successor as praelector of anatomy, Dr. Joannes Deyman, at work in the lecture room. Frederik Ruysch (1638–1731) is a good example of the training and the inspection within the medical profession. On December 22, 1666 he succeeded Dr. Deyman (1620–66) as praelector of anatomy at Amsterdam. On February 6, 1668 he was appointed examiner of midwives, and after the death of Dr. H. van Roonhuysen in 1672 became *stadsvroevaer*. In this post as head of the profession he improved the instruction in medicine for doctors, apothecaries, and midwives. He later took over the *Hortus Botanicus* and had the title Professor of Botany.

Mention should be made of the Remonstrant seminary in Amsterdam, established in 1634 by Simon Episcopius (1583–1643). Not too significant outside religion, the seminary did attract to itself a goodly number of liberal professors and theologians. Among them were Philippe van Limborch (1633–1712), Adam Boreel (1603–66). Stephanus Curcellaeus (1586–1659), and Jean le Clerc (1657–1736). Limborch and Le Clerc were close friends of the English philosopher, John Locke, and had considerable influence on his ideas on theology and toleration.

The two most outstanding Amsterdam contributors to knowledge were both amateurs so far as the academic world was concerned and both were connected with optics. They were of course Anthonie van Leeuwenhoek (1632–1723) and Benedictus de Spinoza (1632–77). Born in the same year the one's name is forever linked with natural science and the other must be considered in any discussion of seventeenth-century philosophy ranging from metaphysics to political science.

Spinoza was the son of a well-to-do merchant who was a Marrano Jew. As a youth he was sent to the Jewish school operated by the Portuguese Jewish community, where he was well grounded in the Hebrew and Arabic classes, and was given private lessons by his parents in Latin, German, and perhaps French and Italian. He learned Spanish and Portuguese, the languages of his parents, at home. His teachers in the Hebrew school included such outstanding Jewish intellectuals as Izaak Aboat, Saul Levi Morteira, and Manasseh ben Israël. After the death of his family, he gave away most of his money to relatives and lived for a time with a former Jesuit, Francis van den Emden, who ran a private school for a living. During that period Spinoza did some teaching and read widely in the works of such neoscholastics as Franco Burgersdijk and Adrianus Heereboord. It was at Emden's school that he was introduced to the philosophy of Descartes.

He was drummed out of the Jewish community because of his unorthodox beliefs. He moved to Rijnsburg where he supported himself by grinding lenses. Patrons such as Simon Joosten de Vries offered him money which he refused. He lived for a while at the home of a surgeon named Hermann Homan and became friendly with the Rijnsburg Collegiants. He met Jean de Witt, and about 1663 moved to Voorburg, just outside the Hague. He died in 1677 of a pulmonary illness brought on from dust inhaled while grinding lenses.

Spinoza in his philosophy tried to construct a system of metaphysics that considered the world as a whole. His god was pantheistic, a conscious omniscient who acted only when it was necessary for him to do so. Man could love God, but should not expect God to love him. These ideas were set out in the *Tractatus Theologico-Politicus*, published anonymously in Amsterdam in 1670. The work raised a hue and cry throughout Europe from Jew and Christian alike. In Amsterdam it was considered a work "forged in hell by a renegade Jew and the Devil, and issued with the knowledge of Mr. Jan de Witt." In the tract Spinoza shows his indebtedness to Descartes.

Spinoza completed the *Ethica* in 1675, and as he had no chance of finding a publisher, he distributed manuscript copies among his friends. He then began the *Tractatus Politicus*, which he did not live to finish. After his death on February 20, 1677, his manuscripts were sent to the Amsterdam publisher, Jan Rieuwertsz. They were edited in secret by his friends Jarig Jelles, Lodewijk Meyer, and G. H. Shiller. By the end of the year, Latin and Dutch versions of his most important writings had appeared. He was buried in the Nieuwe Kerk and later generations recognized him as one of the world's most profound philosophers.

Leeuwenhoek had little formal education in science and was looked down upon by many of his contemporaries because he did not know Latin and because he was by occupation a bookkeeper and cashier for a cloth merchant. Even worse, he was not a doctor of medicine at a time when the medical profession assumed for itself not only a monopoly in the biological sciences but in all learning as well. Leeuwenhoek's findings for these reasons were not well received when they were presented to the Royal Society in England, but his microscope was. Later in life Leeuwenhoek manufactured microscopes. His products and his observations gave man a deeper and wider view into the microcosm just as the telescope had into the macrocosm. He was not without friends. The learned Dr. Reinier de Graaf (1643–73), who was responsible for the discovery of the Graffian follicle, sent Leeuwenhoek's findings to England and encouraged him in his scientific undertakings.

The contributions made to science by that great Amsterdamer were many. Along with the Italian M. Malphigi, he demonstrated the function of the capillaries and thus completed Harvey's theory on the circulation of the blood. In 1674, Leeuwenhoek gave the first accurate description of the red blood corpuscles which he found to be circular in man and oval in frogs and fish. He described and illustrated spermatozoa in dogs and other animals only to be anticipated in this field by a few months by the work of Stephan Hamm. His observations on fermentation in yeast and on bacteria and other "little animals" discovered in drops of water make him practically the founder of bacteriology. As a result of his research many eighteenth-century doctors revived the theory that the presence of invisible animalculae caused certain diseases.

This early microbiologist investigated the structure of dentine, and his researches ultimately led to a description of the sinuses and their relation to the roots of the bicuspids and molars by Highmore, and to a treatise on pyorrhea by the Hollander and part-time Amsterdamer Frederik Ruysch. Leeuwenhoek discovered tartar and the micro-organisms leading to tooth decay; he demonstrated that the human mouth was filled with organisms; and in some ways he was the father of histology, just as he was the first great pioneer in microbiology.

Unlike Spinoza, Leeuwenhoek was recognized in his own lifetime. In addition to Peter the Great, such monarchs as Charles II and George I of England and Frederick I of Prussia visited him. Scientists such as Christiaan Huygens and doctors like De Graaf, Ruysch, Jan Swammerdam, and the illustrious Herman Boerhave came to his door. Professors, doctors, and scientists profited from his findings. He corresponded with the learned of Europe. The Academy of Sciences at Paris made him a member. He remained active intellectually up to his death at age 91, and was buried in the Oude Kerk at Delft in which he had been baptized.

One cannot help being struck by the close connections in Amsterdam among scholars, artists, printers, and booksellers. Not uncommonly the scholar was in the book trade or worked on commission for the publishing houses. In many instances the interplay was the result of family ties. Amsterdam was the book mart of the world, and her ships carried ideas as well as goods to both hemispheres. In the middle of the seventeenth century at Amsterdam there were at least forty printing establishments issuing books in all literary tongues known to Europe. Admittedly the greater part of the output was theological, but that was the market in an age of religious controversy. There was hardly an intellectual or theologian of note that did not have his works appear in Amsterdam. Books that would not be touched elsewhere were accepted by Amsterdam publishers and booksellers, who were not squeamish about violating restrictions on printing because they knew they were rarely enforced. An entire library of Socinian writers sold for a hundred guilders and carried the advertisement in the first volume that the entire eight volume folio set had been ordered burned by the public hangman. A work did not have to agree with the publisher's beliefs.

The Jew Joseph Anthias claimed he had printed so many English Bibles that the dream of Erasmus to have every serving girl and ploughboy own a copy was close to realization. Thomas Hobbes read "bookes of an Amsterdam print," and found the cheap pocket editions of the Elzevier press extremely convenient for reading while he waited on his patron, the Duke of Devonshire.

The first book to be printed in Amsterdam appeared in 1501, the year of a postjubilee indulgence. It was done by Jansz. van Woerden, who printed a number of devotional books as part of the celebration of the papal indulgence. Amsterdam seems to have been the sole city in Holland to have received the indulgence. Another early printer was Doen Pietersz. who began to issue Lutheran Bibles and illustrated religious texts.

During the Eighty Years War, Antwerp began to lose its pre-eminence in printing to Leiden and to Amsterdam. Many book and map stores began to appear along the Damrak. The hardy Dutch mariners who were carrying the Amsterdam flag to all parts of the world purchased the maps for the journey in Amsterdam on the one hand and had their travel accounts printed there on the other. Thus they not only learned geography but contributed to an understanding of it and of cartography as well. In the last quarter of the sixteenth century Amsterdam became the world publishing center for maps, atlases, travel books, and works on navigation and shipbuilding. One of the most significant Amsterdamers so engaged was Cornelis Claeszoon, a publisher who jobbed his printing to several firms. He had the Plantins in Leiden print for him the famous group of nautical charts by Lucas Jansz. Waghenaer, the *Spieghel der Zeevaardt* (1584). This appeared in England in 1588 as *The Mariners Mirrour*, and so useful were Waghenaer's charts to British seamen that the name "Waggoner" became an English synonym for "sea chart."

The increasing demand for maps made the business of cartography profitable. Perhaps the most important geographer in the Low Countries after Mercator was Plancius, who produced in 1592 an important planisphere which is "the first Dutch attempt at a large world map." Plancius never produced an atlas and is therefore not so well known to posterity as many of his contemporaries who extensively used his materials.

Jodocus Hondius (1563–1611), whose place of business was "den wackeren Hont," obtained the plates of Mercator's atlas from his brother-in-law Rumoldus Mercator. In 1606, Hondius began to publish the Mercator-Hondius atlas. He and his successors continued to bring out subsequent editions. The use of the same plates over and over, led to the perpetuation of many mistakes, one of the more famous being the "Island of California." Pieter van den Keere, whose sister married Hondius, engraved for the publisher a set of maps of English countries. Probably through Van den Keere's assistance, Hondius was employed to engrave several of the maps in the folio edition of John Speed's county atlas.

The three great printing establishments in Amsterdam were operated by the Elzeviers, the Janszoons, and the Bleaus. Lodewijk Elzevier (1604–70) came to Amsterdam from Leiden in 1638 to establish a branch print shop. Of Remonstrant sympathies, he was connected with the *Athenaeum Illustre*. He published most of the works of

Descartes, who at the time was not recognized. In 1664, Lodewijk retired, and Daniel Elzevier (1626–80) came from the parent firm in Leiden to take over the business. Shortly the cadet branch outstripped the parent stem. As Professor P. A. Teile-Sichting has pointed out, Daniel Elzevier "conducted his business in the grand style, continually enlarging the circle of his foreign connections, but making many enemies by his obstinacy." He did not shrink from producing large editions: his folio Bibles bound by Albert Magnus were famous; his edition of the *Corpus Juris Civilis* was printed by Bleau and supposedly contained just one typographical error. Elzevier was cosmopolitan. He was the publisher for the French Jansenists and other religious bodies. He recognized the genius and the beauty of the types of Christoffel van Dijk. His catalogue of 1674 contained about twenty thousand items. When he died suddenly in 1680, John Locke wrote: "La mort de monsieur Elzevier est une perte publique." He left his affairs in chaos. His types and presses were sold for approximately 120,000 guilders. Later his book business was also liquidated.

Another printer of note was Johannes Janssonius, whose shop "de Pascaert" was next to Bleau's on the Damrak. Hondius was the brother-in-law of Janssonius and the two merged their establishments. Shortly thereafter Janssonius took over the management, and in 1638 published a new two-volume atlas in his own name. Until 1620, Bleau's customary name was Willem Janszoon (1571–1638), or in its Latin form Gulielmus Janssonius. Because Johannes Janssonius was not above printing his competitor's books under his own name, Bleau added the old by-name of his family and became Willem Jansz. Bleau. Both men published maps and atlases. Justice in the long run triumphed because the house of Bleau outstripped that of Janssonius.

Willem Bleau was indeed a remarkable person. A student of the Danish astronomer, Tycho Brahe, Bleau in 1599 set himself up in business in Amsterdam as a seller of globes, maps, and nautical instruments. He kept abreast of the new geographical discoveries and included them in subsequent editions of his maps. He wrote manuals on seamanship and on theoretical problems in the fields of cartography. Among his many duties was the responsibility of examining navigators. He was not limited to science. He published books by some of the poets of his time: his nephew Hooft, Roemer Visscher, and Vondel. He brought out in a small format a series of texts by classical authors, and printed works in Greek and Arabic. A close friend to Vossius and Barlaeus, he published their works and also many of the writings of Grotius. He became map-maker for the Dutch East India Company, "an important post from the point of view of learning as well as a position of trust, for the Company did not allow publication of maps of the territories that it managed, but kept them secret." He did, however, issue other maps, and in 1634 he and his son Joan brought out a complete two volume atlas of their own.

Three years later father and son opened a new printing office on the Bloemgracht. Here they employed a specialization and a division of labor. There were nine large presses, all of a new design dedicated to the nine muses, and six copper-plate presses for printing maps and engravings. In addition there was a type foundry where founts were cast and presses built. It was a Bleau press that came over on the *Mayflower* with the Pilgrim fathers.

One of the first works printed in the new shop was Vondel's *Gijsbreght von Amstel*, which had been written for the opening of the new theater. In 1638, Willem died and the business fell into the even more capable hands of his son, Dr. Joan Bleau, who was printer to the Swedish royal house and the first printer to become a town councilman and alderman. Joan continued to labor on his father's atlas. Additions and changes were constantly made, and by 1655 there were six volumes. Janssonius by 1662 had enlarged his atlas to eleven volumes. In that same year Bleau began the publication of his *Great Atlas*, the largest and most beautiful atlas that the world has ever seen. The Dutch version was followed by others in Latin, French, and German. A Spanish edition was not finished because a fire in 1672 destroyed Bleau's second printing establishment in the Gravenstraat. Bleau had hoped to publish an illustrated description of the universe complete with nautical and astronomical atlas. The work was never completed, but the famous book on the towns of the Netherlands and the four magnificent volumes on Italy did appear. Bleau had a real fondness for Italy, where he had many connections with people in the world of learning.

Bleau and his father financed their projects by printing missals, prayerbooks, Jesuitical writings and other works for Catholics outside the Netherlands. These were customarily placed on the market in the name of Cologne publishers. The first volume of the *Acta Sanctorum* was in the press when fire leveled the plant on the Gravenstraat. Most Protestants regarded the disaster as a protest from heaven against the printing of Catholic books. The fire loss was 335,000 guilders. Joan died the following year and the firm never recovered. In 1669 its catalogue had contained at least twelve thousand titles. The year 1712 was a bad one for Dutch printing, for at that time the house of Elzevier in Leiden and the house of Bleau in Amsterdam also closed their doors.

The book auction was Dutch in origin. The Dutch Republic in the seventeenth century was not only the country where the most books were printed and published "but might fairly be called the intellectual storehouse of the world." Needless to say Amsterdam had its share of the stores. After he came to Amsterdam, Jean le Clerc began his *Bibliothèque Universelle*. He later wrote: "I confess had (I) lived anywhere else, (I) could not profited so many Volumes, because so many Books are no where so easily publish'd and sold, as at *Amsterdam*."

The next chapter will treat the printing of engravings, music and literature, but two types of printing perhaps should be mentioned at this time: pattern books and news sheets. One could buy books of instruction at Amsterdam on subjects ranging from the design of furniture to military manuals. These pattern books were highly prized abroad by artists and craftsmen. Pepys bought books on ship design for the Royal shipbuilders; others purchased text books. Also in demand were the news letters. Amsterdam was literally the news center of Europe, and the courts of that continent paid as much attention to Amsterdam news courantos as to reports from diplomats. Casper van Hitten's *Courante uyt Italien, Duytsland* ... and his brother Jansz.'s *Tijdinghen uyt Verscheyde Quartieren* were in great demand in England. Approximately sixty to seventy per cent of the news material in the English periodical press originated in the Netherlands, especially in Amsterdam. Time and time again English news publications carried the words "Truthfully translated out of the Low Dutch copies printed at Amsterdam." One of the earliest known newspapers in French was issued by Caspar van Hitten. Also popular were the travel accounts of Jan van Linschoten, Willem Barents, and others, which were put into various tongues and the translations sold all over Europe. Amsterdam was as much a center for the export of knowledge as it was for the stuff of the market place. The city, however, was not just the middle man for culture. The muses of poetry, fine arts, and music were also cultivated in that cosmopolitan European center.

CHAPTER FIVE

Parnassus on the IJ

THE ARTS OF AMSTERDAM in the Golden Century were highly interwoven and often reflected the political, religious, social, and economic currents of the times. In no historical era have literature, painting, and architecture mirrored the life of a single city to such an extent as they did that of Amsterdam during the life spans of Rembrandt and Vondel. The ambivalence in the attitude of the governing classes created an atmosphere which paradoxically supported both a Calvinist state church and the city's most fertile age in art and literature. The town fathers may have on occasion backed the state church against Catholic and Remonstrant, but they were usually limited in their support to the Contra-Remonstrants.

This was especially true in the arts. The *Heeren* forbade the destruction of the church organs, and even went so far as to sponsor concerts on them during which organists such as Jan Pietersz. Sweelinck (1562–1621) played secular music. There may have been no room in Amsterdam for De Keyser's statue of St. John, which he sent to the cathedral at 's Hertogenbosch, but the burghers themselves took over the patronage of artists to a much greater degree than the Roman Church ever had. Private home and public building replaced cathedral and castle as a market for artistic masterpieces. The theater was technically closed and actors were considered second-class citizens, but plays—some with a sharp bite at the Calvinists—could be performed for charitable purposes. During the height of Contra-Remonstrant power, the *Oudemannenhuis* (Old Men's Home) between July, 1615, and April, 1616, enjoyed a net income of 2000 guilders raised mostly from plays by Samuel Coster and Gerbrand Bredero, both bitter critics of the Reformed Church. During the three years that Bredero was associated with the *Oudemannenhuis*, it enjoyed its greatest prosperity. Poetry and prose, some quite earthy and erotic, flourished. The Amsterdamer's zest for life often flouted the Heidelberg Catechism. One cannot help being struck by the great cultural outburst of the period, and by how little store the *Heeren* set by the rigid restrictions that the divines attempted to place upon the city's artistic life.

Dutch is a language not well known to foreigners, so writers using it are limited in their audiences. For that reason Dutch poets and authors through the centuries have labored under a severe disadvantage when it came to gaining recognition outside the Dutch speaking Netherlands. Many of them have written in some other tongue (usually French) to increase their number of readers. In the seventeenth century, however, there was a serious effort made to make Dutch a literary language. Although a number of the old Latinate forms of the Middle Ages were used at that time, many of them were never absorbed into the vernacular as was the case in English. Nevertheless, the literary works of the period are valuable—some even masterpieces. They are, however, difficult to read. Some of them have been translated into better-known tongues to appeal to wider audiences. Others have not. Yet as Adriaan van der Veen has pointed out, "a large audience is not a necessary condition for creating a masterpiece."

Most of the Dutch literature produced in Rembrandt's lifetime is not included in anthologies of world literature and is ignored in university classrooms teaching comparative literature. Some, though certainly not all, works have a real vividness and clarity about them. Pamphlets often overpowering, sometimes coarse and vile, travel accounts, histories, and chronicles have little appeal as literature to the modern reader; "yet the historian's eyes will dispite all discern behind them interesting personalities realizing themselves by their styles." Plays and poems are something else again. Many times the writing is filled with peculiarities, but the patient reader who knows the language will quite often be carried away by its charm, aptness, forcefulness, and beauty.

The many-sidedness of Dutch life made businessmen authors and politicians poets. Many of the literary figures of Amsterdam can be classed as true sons of the Renaissance. Jacob de Graeff, burgomaster, was such a man. He played the lute and the gamba, and in addition to carrying on his official duties, he dabbled in chemistry and in the natural sciences. Behind his house he had a distillery and a laboratory where he conducted experiments with Pieter Jansz. Hooft, doctor and chemist. Along with his helpers he developed a perpetual motion machine and sent that well-known popularizer of science, Cornelis

Drebbel, to demonstrate it before the English court. There were many like De Graeff and Dr. Tulp, whose careers cut across commerce, government, science, and the arts. They provided a milieu for Amsterdam where a variety of views were formed and tastes accepted to a degree never achieved in other Netherlandish cities.

Literature in Amsterdam after the Alteratie did not emerge in full bloom. There can be little doubt that it was influenced by the Italian feeling for beauty, both sensuous and refined, and in the "delight of the realities of human life." Hendrik Spieghel (1549–1612) and Dirk Coornhert (1522–90) were forerunners of the movement, and their philosophical influence was based on the classics. With towering proportions hovered Erasmus with his ideas of free will, the dignity of man, and devotion to classical writers.

Court life played a small role in Dutch literary development. Vondel did receive a golden locket and chain from Queen Christina of Sweden worth $200, and Amelia von Solmo gave him a gold medal for a poem on the marriage of her daughter, Princess Henrietta. He was also rewarded with a silver cup for his ode on the City Hall and was paid in cash for occasional poems celebrating the visits of foreign dignitaries to Amsterdam. Needless to say, it was his business rather than his pen that put bread in his pantry.

Amsterdamers then as now loved occasional poems. By composing such pieces a poet could obtain at least drinking money. In this respect, though on a smaller scale, he was akin to the painter whose portraits and commission pieces fed his family. Caspar Barlaeus, historian and Latin scholar, wrote Latin verse for pay, and defended himself by saying that it hardly behooved a virtuous man to despise an honorable reward, and that a wise man should not be adverse to the glorious gifts of the Gods. For Caspar as for many poets and artists, the gods were the rich burghers of Amsterdam who purchased poems for domestic events such as birthdays, weddings, and funerals. Jan Jansz. Starter, born a Londoner but a Dutch poet of no mean talent, was under contract to twenty young Dutchmen who promised to pay him a weekly stipend of "twelve carolus guilders" on condition that he remain in Amsterdam. Furthermore he was to "give them full access to everything he may make or has made and to write for them poems at three stuivers the page." Vondel was not quite so crass, but for fees he did write many epithalamiums, birthday songs, and elegies. Between 1655 and 1622, at the very pinnacle of his career, he composed five nuptial songs, each of a hundred verses. Writers sometimes worked for publishers as editors, or wrote occasional verse for them for a pittance. They could usually expect that their major works would be pirated.

A highly formative force in Dutch literature was the traditions of the chambers of rhetorics which under Burgundian rule had flourished throughout the Low Countries. Amsterdam's chamber called both the "Old Chamber" and *Eglantier* (flourishing of love), had a long and successful existence which continued into the seventeenth century. A second chamber was formed after the influx of the Brabanters. Called *'t Wit Lavender* (white lavender), it was not of much significance except that at one time Vondel was a member. Later he joined the Eglantier. At the beginning of the seventeenth century Pieter Hooft wrote a poem about the Eglantier entitled *Parnassus on the IJ*:

One finds that Amsterdam with its poetic heights
The obscure way to praise and virtue lights;
And Kampen, whose art in general run of things
The praise of virtue and the curse of vice does sing.
Vondel, Bredero, Victorijn and Coster
Will harmony and tune forever foster.

At that time Spieghel was the leader of the Amsterdam Chamber. Also highly active was Cornelis van Kampen (1564–1623), nephew of Roemer Visscher (1547–1620), but as a Netherlandish author Kampen is not so well known as was Joan Vechters commonly called Victorijn. Visscher himself did yeoman service for the Chamber, which often met at his house. This merchant's salon up to his death was a favorite gathering place for the wits and talents of the city, second only to Hooft's evenings at Muiden Castle. Erasmus was the spiritual ancestor of this Libertine who disliked the affectations of the phrase mongers and the zeal of the fanatics. His *Sinnepoppen* (1614), an emblem book, has stood the test of time better than some of his other writings. He worked to keep the Dutch language from being defiled by foreign mannerisms. This "Dutch Martial" was no austere moralist: "Not the trespass of his fellow men, but their false pretences, not the joy of life, but the denial of its joys were the butts of his sarcasm." Vondel catches the mood of the Visscher drawing room:

Let fall the anchor. Here the flood is stilled.
Here is neither ebb nor tide. Here no unrest.
I take my way to blissful Roemer's house,
Whose floor is walked, whose threshold crossed
By painters, artists, singers, poets.

In addition to Visscher's group and the Muiden Circle, there were countless homes in Amsterdam where music, poetry, and discussion of the arts were at given times the order of the evening, but the quality of such salons was naturally uneven.

The Eglantier split over the efforts of Hooft, Bredero, and Coster to popularize the vernacular and to resist the flowery Renaissance classicism which was permeating the Dutch language. Coster's Academy was in the forefront of a squabble that eventually closed the Chamber. At odds with the "moderns" was the gifted Dirk Rodenburg (1578–1644). He was Antwerp born, and almost alone among the literary Amsterdamers, sided with the Contra-Remonstrants, although he may have taken that position more because of his dislike of Coster than because of any deep religious convictions. His bombastic plays did not outlive his own century, but both he and Coster by their personalities "helped to create an atmosphere in which the great ones breathed."

The theater was the arena in which the Dutch language made its strongest challenge to the Latinists. This is understandably so because the chambers of rhetorics during the Middle Ages enjoyed a long tradition by which one town competed against another to see which guild could present the best dramatic production. These contests, called *Landjuweel* (County Jewel), were accompanied by guild processions, theatrical performances, banquets, and the awarding of prizes. Plays dealing with biblical subjects were similar to the miracle plays of the Middle Ages. But the Calvinists frowned on all such activities and considered the chambers to be little more than societies of poets, rhymsters, and literary dilletantes, "who in their meetings worshipped both Bacchus and Apollo." The clergy commonly and derisively called chamber members *rederijkers kannekijkers* (eloquent poets look-in-the-pot).

The medieval mystery play was transformed by Vondel into a classical drama in the style of Seneca "enlivened by *tableaux vivants* and the musical accompaniment of the chorus." Romantic drama was preferred by the groundlings because of its realism and its unrestrained production of horrors. Plays with classical themes, but loaded with political overtones, such as Coster's *Iphigenia* and Vondel's *Palamedes*, were the talk of the town and the cross of the government. On the whole the Amsterdam theater was much more politically oriented than the drama produced at the Blackfriars and the Globe. The farce (*klucht*), such as Bredero's *Spanish Brabanter*, which satirized customs, foibles, and daily life in general, was popular as was comedy (*blijspel*) such as Hooft's *Warenar*, wherein a work of Plautus became a burlesque of Amsterdam life.

Adam Karels could command five guilders for a performance, but the going rate for actors was three. As there were approximately only ninety days of theater a year, acting was hardly a lucrative profession. Men played female parts until the middle of the century, when foreign actresses began to come into Amsterdam. Among the early native actresses were Adriana van den Berg, Elizabeth Kalbergen, and Susanna Eckhout. Traveling players from England toured Amsterdam and performed sometimes on the squares and sometimes in hired halls. The acting profession as a whole was held in low esteem, and in "the late eighteenth century players were still disqualified as witnesses in court on the ground that they belonged to a disreputable calling." Admission to a performance was about three stuivers.

The theater served a real purpose. It provided intellectual stimulation and showed the uses of the Dutch language. Throughout the first part of the century there was a constant struggle between the Eglantier and Coster's Academy, where the more controversial and better plays were produced. A permanent theater under the patronage of the burgomasters was inaugurated in 1637, and the first performance was of Vondel's *Gysbreght*. Today the theater season in Amsterdam opens annually with that historic play. As a sop to ministerial opposition, all proceeds from the new playhouse were earmarked for charity.

Although the intellectual and literary greats had many of their most important works produced at the city playhouse, it would be a mistake to think that they dominated that theater. One of the smash hits of the time was written by Jan Vos, an illiterate glazier; that bloody melodramatic monstrosity entitled *Aran and Titus* numbered among its most enthusiastic admirers the humanist Barlaeus. Vos eventually became director of the theater and pandered to the current taste for elaborate spectacles and ingenious stage material. In the words of an enthusiastic admirer: "So now the eye as well as the ear will have its share in what is being played."

Except for Jacob Cats and Constantijn Huygens, Holland's chief literary figures during its Golden Age resided in Amsterdam. Cats and Huygens are better known to English-speaking readers than are Hooft, Bredero, and Vondel partly because Cats's emblem books were widely circulated in England and because Huygens, son of a world renowned scientist, besides his own writings translated poems of John Donne into Dutch. So far as literary significance is concerned, the three leading Amsterdam poets surpass Cats and Huygens, and along with Coster made more far-reaching contributions to the Dutch language. Perhaps brief sketches of Coster, Hooft, Bredero, and Vondel will provide some insights into Amsterdam's preponderant position in Dutch literature during the age of Rembrandt.

Coster was the son of a carpenter who had come to Amsterdam as a refugee during the time of troubles. He took a degree in medicine at Leiden, and sometime shortly after 1610 he became Amsterdam's city physician, a post he held until his death about 1664. Coster brought with him from Leiden a five-act play entitled *Boereklucht van Teeuwis de Boer en Menjuffrouw van Grevenlinckhuysen* (Peasant Farce of Teeuwis the Farmer and My Lady Grevenlinckhuysen), which was played in 1612 at the *Eglantier*. Based on an old folk song from an Antwerp song book, the work related the story of how a clever farmer who looked stupid cheated a noble lady and her husband. The next year he came up with another five-act play, *Tysken van de Schilden*, whose plot also came out of the Antwerp song book. Both these early plays were written in doggerel *(knippelversen)*, but in 1615 he brought out *Itys*, written in Alexandrine verse and based on the Greek classic. Van der Passe printed this for Coster and in the same year published *De Rijcke Man*, which Coster did on behalf of a lottery to raise money for one of the Amsterdam poor houses. These early works were marked with the rhetorical style of the chambers. Of more significance was his *Iphigenia* (1617). Under the guise of a Greek fable and writing in the style of Seneca, Coster held the Contra-

Remonstrants up to satire and warned that Calvinist tyranny was no better than Roman popery.

Coster is best known for his Academy. Although it failed as an educational institution and became little more than a theater, it was highly influential so far as the Dutch language was concerned. Both Hooft and Bredero backed Coster's attempts to popularize the use of Dutch in teaching and in literature. Hooft continually fought the adoption in the language of foreign innovations, and "dared to pick up the plastic, the colourful word, the idiomatic phrase out of the gutter." Hooft wrote Huygens in 1630: "To pick up outcast words off the street and make them do such service as they are fit for, even though it were among the nobility is a thing one can take credit for." It is unfortunate that Hooft did not always take his own advice: his formal writings are far too often based on Latin models. Yet he and his circle helped to fashion Dutch as a light tool for exquisitely courteous intercourse both spoken and by correspondence.

Bredero went farther than Hooft when it came to using the vernacular in its most realistic manner. In the preface of the *Groot Lied-Boeck (Great Song Book)* he boasted: "Fat lot do I care whether I learn my mother-tongue from a mighty king or from beggar." To Bredero it made scant difference if the words he used came out of the "rubbish bin" or from the greatest literature of the world. As he said (though he starts out with a falsehood): "I have read no book but the book of general use. . . . I have done my utmost to express my boorish jokes in the sweetest boorish words." How Bredero abided by his own precepts will be illustrated below.

The struggle to resist foreign idioms was a difficult one.

There was a considerable amount of Dutch verse written in the French Renaissance manner as is indicated by a miscellany of Dutch poetry, *Den Bloem-Hof van de Neder-landsche Jeught* (The Flower Garden of Netherland Youth), which first appeared in 1608. Hooft was the first Dutch poet to go beyond imitating the French Renaissance style. His first play, *Archilles ende Polyxena* (*c.* 1598), was composed when he was sixteen and before he embarked upon a two-year tour of Italy, where he spent most of his time in Florence. There a view of his own poetic power was revealed to him, but his mind remained true to the genius of Holland, where "Fame's summit can be climbed by the steep Stairs of Integrity." Spieghel showed him the way to a personal philosophy in which the faith of the Erasmian Christian given him by his father was channeled into a form of Stoic determinism "which embraced all the moral principles of Christianity but lacked its religious fervor." With Hooft, tolerance, love, awe of God, Italian humanism, and sensuousness were merged into a single entity like that of the figures in a Rembrandt painting.

Hooft's dramatic writings represented the full Dutch Renaissance. His initial work was followed by *Thesus en Adraine* (*c.* 1602) and *Granida* (1605), both composed before he was twenty. The plays were a blend of Seneca and the French dramatic form and had many fluent and mellow lines. *Granida* is the best of the three, and its characters have a real personality, though Hooft is remembered primarily as a dramatist of ideas. As Professor Theodoor Weevers observed: "As a romantic drama, *Granida* is a brilliantly written failure; its dramatic interest lies in the fact that it was an attempt, if an immature one, at the form in which Hooft was later to achieve mastery, the allegorical drama of ideas."

Daniel Heinsius revealed to Hooft the possibilities in that genre, which Hooft crystallized in the tragedy *Geeraerdt van Velsen*, a play treating the revolt against Floris V by Geeraerdt van Velsen, Herman van Woerden, and Gijsbrecht van Aemstel. In another drama, *Baeto,* Hooft tried to create a national myth by embodying in the corporate personality of Baeto and his followers the essential qualities of the Dutch nation. Of special interest was the dramatist's use of Greek style choruses. For example, in the *Geeraerdt*, "the personified River Vecht then comforts the Chorus of Amsterdam Maidens with a prophecy of the glory of seventeenth-century Amsterdam."

His best known play, the comedy *Warenar*, or *Ware-nar*, was presented anonymously in Coster's Academy the day after it opened. The work is based on the *Aulularia* by Plautus and has lasted through the centuries. It pokes fun at the daily life of the Amsterdamer as it depicts the attempts of the penny-pinching Warenar to find some quiet in his life after he finds a pot of gold under the floor of his house. In some of his writings Hooft was quite bawdy, but never to the extent of Huygens or Bredero. *Trijntje Cornelisdr.-Klucht*, his comedy or farce about Trijntje Cornelisdaughter, the wife of a Dutch skipper, shows him at his most earthy moments.

It was in lyric poetry that Hooft excelled, and his genius gave a style and purity of tone to the Dutch language never before achieved. His occasional verse fitted into the life of Amsterdam. At the request of Hendrik de Keyser, he wrote the famous proverb which begins "Fear not I bear you no malice" for the sculptor's statuary "Chastisement and Punishment" in the Spinhuis, a corrective institution for wayward women. He did the inscription for Heemskerck's tomb in the Oude Kerk and wrote a welcoming ode for the arrival of the "Daughters of Great Britain," when British royalty visited Amsterdam on May 25, 1613.

His love songs and love poems still charm the reader. Hooft took his love life seriously, and a knowledge of his erotic development is necessary for an understanding of his poetry and his character. Spieghel, an old friend of the family, said that Hooft in 1602 was leading a fruitless existence because his chief concern was with affairs of the heart. Spieghel thought that Hooft might curb his restlessness by reading Montaigne. At the time Hooft seems to have been in love with Brechtje, the daughter of Jan Spieghel, and the affair seems to have been terminated by outside pressure. Brechtje probably committed suicide. Hooft's poem *Het Daget in Den Oosten* bemoans their separation. Roughly translated it goes:

After this hour I shall never more enjoy
The friendship of your eyes, the lustfulness of your mouth.

The friendship of your eyes, the lustfulness of your mouth
The secrets of your heart that before me open stood
But nonetheless I am your slave throughout eternity

Other women who prompted his muse were Brechtje's sister Anna, Ida Quekels, and A. B., who perhaps was the daughter of Burgomaster Boelens.

His most passionate poems were for Christina van Erp, whom he married May 23, 1610. She became his hostess at Muiden, where he resided as Sheriff of Muiden, Bailiff of Gooiland, and Head Officer of Weesp. Hooft at Muiden

Castle and at his winter home in Amsterdam, 65 Keizers-gracht, gathered together artists and wits. Among those who came to read poetry, discuss affairs and philosophy, and to listen to music were Grotius, Bredero, Coster, the daughters, Maria ("Tesselschade") and Anna of Roemer Visscher, the singer Francisca Duarte, Casper van Barlaeus, Huygens, Laurens Reael (at one time Governor-General in the East Indies), Laurens Baeck, and the Catholic poet Cornelis Gijsbertsz. Plemp. Vondel joined them on rare occasions, but was not one of the inner circle. Other lovers of poetry who went to Muiden were George Rataller Doublet, Jacob van der Burgh, John van Brosterhuysen, and Johan van Heemskerk. The latter was the author of the famous *Arcadia* along with many love songs.

Among the luminaries was Maria "Tesselschade" Visscher, who went by her nickname meaning "Texel damage" given to her by her father because on the night of her birth he lost a ship off Texel. Although her sister Anna Visscher was skillful with brush and needle, an engraver on glass and author of emblematic verse, Tesselschade was more talented and more worldly. She inspired Hooft, Huygens, Bredero, and others to write about her. She herself wrote good poetry and was an excellent translator. She was the best songstress at Muiden Castle. To Hooft, gold looked like dross and diamonds like glass when she came into a room. To him and others she was the light of Holland, the second wonder of the world. Bredero wooed her in her youth and Barlaeus and Huygens courted her in her widowhood. Hugyens wrote an elegy for this charmer:

> *Here Tesselschade lies.*
> *Let no one rashly dare*

To weigh the measure of her worth
Which was beyond compare.
Her glory like the sunny skies
The effort of the poets defies.

The Muiden circle increased its activities after Hooft's second marriage, which was to Helconora Hellemans, and continued to attract talent to it down to 1647. Joannes Vollenhove (1632–1708), whom Vondel called his "son in the art," wrote:

At Muiden was the true Helicon
And Hooft Apollo on a castle set . . .

This golden time must Holland n'ere forget.

One of Hooft's best poems to his wife compares his rapture on beholding her beauty with the ecstasy of the blind boy to whom Christ gave the power to see. Hooft was genuine and serious in his passions; and except for the death of his wife, which stunned him, the poet was usually able to keep his feelings under intellectual control. Many of his poems — as was the custom — were intended to be set to existing music. Thus some of his finest songs are playful but restrained. "Hooft seems to dance on the surface of life like a skater on a deep frozen lake; one marvels at his airy grace while sensing hidden depths of passion." To him God was the source of all life and beauty, and God gave man love to cherish and to enjoy. True to his wives, Hooft enjoyed nevertheless the society of cultivated women, but he was always a Dutchman with much homely humor and an abundance of common sense. His poems, elegant and musical, vary in form and rhythm, and at

times are touched with a passion warmed always by a
sensuous love of song and women.

Two sonnets translated by experts will illustrate the
genius of Hooft. The first is from Professor Barnouw's
Coming After and the second from Professor Weevers'
*Poetry of the Netherlands in Its European Context 1170–
1930.*

Sonnet One

My love, my love, thus spoke my love to me
While on her delicate lips my lips were browsing.
Those words, too clear to be in need of glorizing,
Entered my ears and stirred mysteriously.

My inmost thoughts into tumultuous stress,
They did not trust the ear and, at their pressure,
I begged my dearest for a fuller measure
Of that confession, and she did confess.

Oh bounty of the heart that overflows!
Entranced, each heart did other's heart imprison,
But when the morning star fled for the risen
Light of the sun, the sad truth too arose.

Oh Gods, how close are things that are and seem
How like the dream is life, like life the dream.

Sonnet two

When by the world's blest Light the youth who was born
  blind
Was given sight, he stood in wonder and amazed;
Movement of colour, shape of plant, of man, of beast,
O'erwhelmed his very thought and even speech con-
  strained;

And then those castles, towers almost sky-high upraised,
— The time-beguiling of man's enterprising mind —
But the visible God, the Sun, majestic reigned.
His tongue was dumb; the heart with countless tongues
  had praised!

Verily thus, my Light, when you appear to me,
And when my soul revealed can your soul's beauty see
By eyesight of the heart that years yourself to meet,
Then fills my heart with joy and admiration rife
And gratitude towards you and Him who gave you life
Until it bursts and droppeth broken at your feet.

In addition to emblem poetry, epithalamium, and occasional poetry, Hooft also wrote poems of a reflective nature, for "he was a political and ethical thinker as well as a lover." Two of the best of this type are his famous pen-portrait of Montaigne and a sonnet on the birth of a child to his brother, who at the time resided in London. Sir Herbert Grierson has superbly rendered the latter into English:

O fair young fruit, that from the quiet night
Of slumber in the womb awaked must go —
Time that lets nothing rest hath willed it so —
Forth to the whirl of sense and realms of light,
Now has birth given thee o'er to Fortune's might.
Her school is changed. She mingles joy with woe,
Sorrow with joy; exalts and hurls below,
Till dazed with hope and fear we darkling fight.
May He who giveth all things grant thee a heart
Undaunted to withstand the fiercest dart
Hate in her anger at thy life may speed;

Her gifts too, when in milder mood she pours
Riches and joys and honours in full stores,
Be it thine to use grateful, but with good heed!

Hooft devoted the middle and later years of his life to
the writing of history, and as Professor Pieter Geyl says
"in this work he carried the culture of his time to a high
pinnacle." Early he did a biography of Henry IV of France
which appeared in 1626. A second work, *De Rampzalighe-*
den der Verheffing van den Huize Medicis (The Wretch-
edness of the Rise of the Medicis), was not published until
after his death. His masterpiece of twenty-seven books
deals with Netherlands history. Twenty volumes cover the
period from the abdication of Charles V to the death of
Prince William, and seven more treat the United Provinces under Leicester. Hooft's history was based on a wide
knowledge of the literature from both the rebel and Spanish sides and on family papers and traditions. His observations were subtle and clear. According to Professor Geyl:
"History proper, had not been written in Dutch, but in
Hooft's *History* the chronicle form . . . is completely left
behind. The power of description is maintained on a rare
level; no matter where one opens the book it lives." The
interpretation is in harmony with the ideas of the aristocratic and Libertine class to which Hooft belonged. Liberty was something to be defended from the bigotry of the
fanatic and the stupidity of the mob as well as from foreign
despots and their agents.

Unfortunately Hooft did not transfer his light and
vivid style to his historical writings. Tacitus was his idol,
and he had translated the *Annals,* the *History,* and other
smaller works of Tacitus not once but twice — first literal-

ly and then somewhat more freely. His close adherence to Tacitus as a model makes his historical works extremely difficult reading. Hooft deserves the title "the Dutch Tacitus," but the designation in this case is not necessarily complimentary.

Bredero considered Hooft the outstanding poet of his time. His poems were giant strides forward in Dutch literature. He made his home a focal point for the dissemination of Dutch culture. He befriended poets and artists, and above all he was a champion of liberty. On the other hand he was always the aristocrat, and he lacked the feeling for the people that Bredero and Vondel had. He died on May 24, 1647. With his passing a void was created in Amsterdam's cultural life. The salons of his successors never equaled his and Visscher's.

When one thinks of Amsterdam art in the seventeenth century, especially painting, one calls to mind "the mysterious chiaroscuro" of Rembrandt's later period; the peaceful and shimmering landscapes of Esaias van de Velde (c. 1599–1630), Jacob Ruysdael (1629–82), or Meindert Hobbema (1638–1709); and the realism of Thomas de Keyser (1596/7–1667), Nicolaes Maes (1634–93) or Bartholomeus van der Helst (1613–70). One rarely thinks of the baroque pieces of Pieter Lastman (1583–1633), Nicolaes Moyaert (1592/3–1655), or for that matter Gérard de Lairesse (1640–1711). And who can write Dutch social history without making reference to the works of Adriaan van Ostade (1610–84), Jan Steen (1626–79), Pieter de Hooch (1629–84), and Jan Vermeer (1632–75)?

And so it was also in lyrical poetry. The allegorical works of the poets of the *Bloem-Hof* became curiosities of literature. "The glory of the Dutch lyric is the so-called *gezel-*

schapslied." These were the songs of the people at parties, weddings, picnics, homes, inns, and brothels; the songs of the people in the Warmoestraat or in the Nes, by the open stalls on the market place, and in the haunts of fishermen and seamen. Professional and amateur poet set to verse the old tunes of the time — some Dutch, some English, and others French or Italian. "The chief representatives of this genre are Hooft, Bredero, and Starter; Vondel also wrote a number. . . . in their more personal lyrics they all tried their hand at baroque forms, the coming literary fashion, with varying success. But the living tradition of the Dutch *gezelschapslied* was so strong that the poets instinctively harked back to the Renaissance manner as soon as they wrote to music."

Bredero, who signed his name Breero, was the Breughel of Amsterdam literature. There is no doubt that he is the most thoroughly Dutch in his literary output, because he sought beauty in every aspect of Dutch life — in the tavern, in the country, and in the city. He left a volume of lyrical verse and a collection of comedies and farces "that form the best literary counterpart of the work of the Dutch genre painters." The discovery of beauty at home was the outstanding achievement of Bredero and the genre painters. They dared to be themselves and "showed foreigners the way to unsuspected sources of artistic inspiration."

Bredero, born in 1585, dwelt in the Nes next to St. Pieterskapel, which had been converted into a butcher shop after the Alteratie. On its top floor the Eglantier held its meetings. His father was a lesser burgher, who made shoes, dealt in leather goods, and held minor civic posts. A man of some means, he bought a house in 1602 on the Oude-Zijdsvoorburgwal by the Varkenssluis, and when he died left an estate of nearly 15,000 guilders. It was in this house that Bredero lived until his death in 1618. The young poet courted Tesselschade, often visited Hooft at Muiden, was a member of the Eglantier, and bore a standard in the *schutterij*. He was a friend to Coster, Daniel Heinsius, and perhaps Grotius. Throughout his brief but active life, he moved among the leading intellectuals of Amsterdam. His strength and reputation, however, were primarily based on his understanding of the people of Amsterdam: the small tradesman or the laborer; the farmer who lived outside the city walls who came in by *trekschuit* (boat pulled along the canal) to peddle his wares. Like Steen, Ostade, and Teniers, Bredero had a real feeling for the lower classes and could laugh lustily with them or at them.

He received instruction at one of the better schools in Latin, Greek, Dutch, and French. Later he described himself as "a bad Amsterdamer who had but a little French bumping about his head." He championed the language of Waterland and old Amsterdam and claimed that his mother tongue was worth more to him than gold, silver, or copper coins. His knowledge of the classics and French, in which he was proficient enough to write a sonnet, added rhythm and grace to his verse. Much of his drama is sonorous, bombastic, and jingling. He was unable to reach the new harmony of the true Dutch Renaissance poet as personified by Hooft, but he could and did develop his natural style of direct self-expression and stark realism. In his own style he was the consummate master. At the time of his death on August 23, 1618, he was in many ways a much more accomplished dramatist and poet than either Hooft or Vondel were at the same age, thirty-three.

Bredero had been a painter before he became a poet. He had studied under Francesco Badens (1571–1618), an artist very much under the influence of the Venetian school. Bredero's approach to poetry was direct. He boasted no other book but that of language usage, and he apologized with mock humility for any errors he might have committed "through ignorance of outlandish tongues. For I have as a painter been guided by the painters' maxim that the best artists are those who come nearest to life." Through traveling English players in Amsterdam, Bredero was familiar with the works of Ben Jonson, Christopher Marlowe, and Shakespeare. Their influence along with Renaissance overtones can be seen in Bredero's drama just as the songs of English madrigal singers and dancers who performed on Amsterdam streets are reflected in his lyrics. Bredero's voice is more bawdy than those of the English dramatists and his use of folk diction is more graphic. His dramatic ability to delineate a character almost on first appearance on stage amounted to genius.

A good example of this is in *The Spanish Brabanter*. Robbeknol, the servant of Jerolimo the Brabanter, gives his life history in his opening lines. His Friesland father deserted to Spain, and his Alkmaar mother poisoned the traitor. She then came to Amsterdam, where she bought a small house, "Den Graaf van Embden." She made a living by taking in washing and drying the clothes in the nearby open fields. One day a Negro servant brought in his master's laundry for her to do.

> *He was an ugly Nigger and she was attractive*
> *Yes, even handsome. Fooy when a woman's green*
> *She'd sleep with hangman, dog, or devil.*

My mom a widow was with hot quick blood
And knew the joys of screwing well.
What did she do? She laid the blackamoor
To prove if Moors were soft as she was told,
But what he filled her with was hard as nails.
So she gave him a pretty little blacky.

After that the Moor lived with the family for a couple of years and the youth became rather fond of him. Then the authorities found about the affair and tried and punished Moor and mother. Robbeknol was sent to an orphanage. He escaped, did odd jobs, and finally came into the service of the Brabanter. All that in an entry!

Bredero's first play *Rodd'rick ende Alphonsus* was played in the Eglantier in 1611. Except for some autobiographical references, the play was little value. The *Griane*, given in 1612 on the Sunday before Christmas, was more realistic and was perhaps influenced by Robert Greene's *Pandosto* or Shakespeare's *The Winter's Tale*. Bredero's three best known farces are *Van de Koe* (Of the Cow), *Symen Sonder Soeticheyt* (Simon Without Sweetness), and *Van den Molenaer* (The Miller's Play). They were printed by Van der Passe in 1619 along with the farce, *Van de Hoogduytsche Quacksalvar* (The German Quack), which Dr. A. A. van Rijnback attributes also to Bredero. These farces have tremendous realism and illustrate Bredero's superb talent for humor—sometimes earthy but usually comical.

His compositions for the stage show him to be a master in the use of dialect (*volkstaalvirtuoos*) and in the writing of short popular plays (*volkstooneeltjes*). *The Spanish Brabanter* is without doubt Bredero's best dramatic work, and it ranks alongside Vondel's *Lucifer* as one of the best pieces of Dutch dramatic literature produced in the seventeenth century. In *The Brabanter* Bredero turned aside from the Franco-Spanish-Italian conventual and aristocratic models and looked inward to the Holland that he knew and to the homely and the genuine that he could depict so well.

Unlike Coster, Bredero did not deliberately reject the religious and moral ideas of Calvinism. He had inner misgivings about his faith and some of his religious poems are sober and introspective. Yet in *The Brabanter* Bredero did lash out at the Calvinists from the South Netherlands, whose ideas, airs, and graces he judged to be superficial and hollow. His conception of Jerolimo is the attitude of the Amsterdam libertine toward the Brabanters, some of whom were the central core of the Contra-Remonstrant party. In the play, Bredero championed a native art with deep roots as opposed to the somewhat tired veneer left over from the Burgundian-Spanish inheritance.

Even more important, the play is a masterful canvas of life itself. In it the author gives full rein to his artistic cravings to come closer to reality albeit crude in many of its aspects. He scanned the rude, licentious, swiftly developing society around him and saw its vices and virtues. The characters he put in the play are varied and present a broad cross section of his own Amsterdam. In addition to the *Jonker* Jerolimo and his servant Robbeknol, there are a person whose job is to keep dogs out of the church, some patriots, three spinsters, a landlord, goldsmith, painter, and clerk, a sheriff and his rogues, a neighbor, a dealer in second hand clothes, and a pawn broker. It is Bredero at his best and in the genre of his day. Another excellent example of Bredero depicting the scenes of his time can be found in *Het Moortje* (The Little Moor), an Amsterdam version of *The Eunuchus* by Terence. Bredero takes his reader along the Dam and the Nes to visit the guild halls of the butchers, the fresh vegetable markets, and of course the stalls of the fishmongers. The sights and sounds and almost the smells of the Amsterdam streets come off the printed pages. How much more effective the plays must have been when given on the stage!

It was in lyrical verse that Bredero was at his best. He was a true poet of the Renaissance, but without an official philosophy. He inclined toward Christian humanism, and in his lyrics he sought to look introspectively into the corners of his own heart. He also wrote songs about the life around him, songs of the city, and songs about the farmers and the travelers he encountered on his frequent trips to Haarlem. He was obviously very close in spirit to the genre artists in poems such as *A Peasant's Party*, wherein a group of country bumpkins join in a goose pull party with peasants from another village with all sorts of surprises for all:

> But Matthew and Katie, that sweet and simple lass
> Those two sneaked together into the new-mown grass
> Not to say morning mass!
> You know the game, it is ever the same
> I thought it was a farce.

A tumble in the hay may have been a farce to Bredero but not love. It is as the poet of love that he is best remembered; his songs still live. He followed the courtly approach in style and diction necessary for a poet of his day, but his freshness and his spontaneity make his verse timeless. In rhythm, and sound, his voice was richer and more

lyrical than those of his contemporaries. He was one of
the most beautiful songsters in Dutch history.

He was more successful with his poems than with his
women, though one must admit that in his short life he
was only lonely between loves, which incidentally were
periods of extremely short duration. Bredero loved life and
he loved love. He burned inside with wild unquenchable
fires of sensuousness, and his Odyssey seeking that one perfect love can be charted in his verse. First there was Margriete who between 1611 and 1615 crowded everything
else out of his mind and body. He was moved deeply by
her great beauty and wrote twelve lovely sonnets to her,
Van de Schoonheydt (On Beauty). These were part of a
collection of verse which appeared in 1615 under the title
Apollo of Gesangh der Musen (Apollo or Songs of the
Muse). Included also were a collection of poems, *Klagte
van Cupido* (Complaints of Cupid), written by his close
friend Jan Jansz. Starter, the poet who came nearest to
equaling his song.

Other women followed. There was an "intelligent"
widow, whom Bredero called *"May Aaltje"* and then Tesselschade Visscher of the Muiden circle. After a few stop-
gaps he came to the greatest love of his life, Magdalena
Stockman, whom he loved and lost between the appearance of *The Spanish Brabanter* and his early death. She
married just before he died, and his swan song to verse,
the lovely *Ooghen vol Majesteyt* (Eyes Full of Majesty),
was written for her.

In his love poems Bredero used many of the motifs of
the Middle Ages: the complaints of a woman about the
physical impotency of her husband, of the problems of an
old man married to a young woman and vice versa, and

the usual trials and tribulations to which the true lover is subjected. The poems are realistic, lustful, jubilant, and light-hearted, especially those in the *Boertigh Liedt-Boek* (Peasants' Songbook). In the *Groote Bron der Minnen* (Great Source of Love) and the *Amoreus Liedt-Boek* (Song-Book of Love), he alternately rejoices and complains about his affairs of the heart. He revels in sensuousness and delight on the one hand and is filled with jealousies and despairs on the other. After his usual defeat, his verse becomes filled with complaints and guilt feelings, and he becomes inconsolably disenchanted with the futilities of this world. But not for long. He, "with refreshing disregard of the accepted amourous conventions of the day," expatiates "on the perplexities of the lover too changeable to serve only one mistress. And, transparently, he tries to deceive himself and others by dwelling on the delightful thought of the unlimited possibilities open to him—for are there not as good fish in the sea as come out of it?"

His works were published twice without his permission. The first known official edition was brought out in Amsterdam in 1621 by Cornelis van der Passe. This was actually a fourth printing and was entitled *Geestigh Liedt-Boecxken* (Witty Songbook). The most famous collection of his poems entitled *Boertigh, Amoreus en Endachtigh Groot Liedboeck* (The Great Songbook of Peasant, Love, and Serious Songs) was issued the next year by Van der Passe. That was one of the great events in both poetry and music because the name of the accompanying tune was included with the poem. Two examples of his delicacy and craft are below. The first is a sonnet translated by Professor Barnouw, who has skillfully caught its grace and beauty:

Blest is the comb of gilded ivory
That serves, and does deserve, to stroke those tresses.
More blest the net entangling in its meshes
Together with her braids the soul of me.
Yet would I rather see them wave at will.
The skill of art must yield to nature's skill.

Professor Weevers has done one of Bredero's *Adieu-Liedt*, songs of parting. This last stanza is typical:

All that a man can think of
To wish his friend, to wish his dearest love,
That would I sweeting, give you,
Were it God's will the same to me to give.
Ah, think of me,
As I of thee
With eager-hearted yearning;
Yea, all my thoughts
Now long with passion's force
For your returning.

As Bakhuizen van den Brink, an able mid-nineteenth-century archivist and scholar, remarked: "Bredero and his successors will never die so long as the art collections show the works of Jan Steen and de Ostade to strip away our pruderies and to speak to us a language before which our ears are not for a single moment numbed."

Bredero may have been the poet of the people of Amsterdam, but the poet laureate of the city was Vondel. It is impossible to find in all cultural history a poet and a city more closely intertwined. Both rose to great heights together. The poet loved Amsterdam and Amsterdam loved its poet. Vondel in one of his more famous sonnets placed an imperial crown on the city on the IJ. In 1653 the artists and writers of his city crowned Vondel at St. Luke's Guild as chief of Dutch poets, an honor that the years have failed to eradicate.

Vondel was much more closely associated with Amsterdam than ever Shakespeare was with London. In countless poems, Vondel praised the city, its harbors, its walls, its orphanages, the exchange, the theater, the East India House, the City Hall, the trade, the buildings, the town fathers, and every phase of Amsterdam life. If as Goethe claimed the occasional poem is the best, then Vondel was the poet par excellence. He celebrated the arts of his time. He was the friend of musician and painter, preferring the idealism of the Italian school to the realism of a Steen or Ostade or the revolutionary splendor of Rembrandt. He brought his gift of poetry to the city, and he found the city of his adoption worthy of his great talents. In no other milieu could his genius have soared to such heights. He transformed the great tragedies of the classics to historical accolades of Amsterdam. As Professor Brugsmans has so truly stated: "It is not possible to comprehend Vondel without Amsterdam, just as it is impossible to comprehend Amsterdam without Vondel."

Vondel surpassed all Dutch poets with his versatility, the scope and profundity of his thought, and his fantastic command of all metrical forms with the exception of the sonnet. Even in writing sonnets, he was second only to Hooft. Admittedly some critics feel that Vondel was too much bound by French and Italian conventions. To be sure he did employ those methods. Like Shakespeare he also drew his plots from the classics and history. Unlike the great English poet, Vondel found inspiration for his drama in the Bible. He was the best poet the Netherlands ever produced, and he was paramount in nearly all genres. Like many geniuses of giant stature, he suffered terribly at the hands of lesser imitators.

His life profoundly influenced his poetic growth. His love of Amsterdam in part stemmed from the fact that the city had given his refugee father economic opportunity and had put an end to his running. His early poems were highly rhetorical because he belonged to the Brabant Chamber of Rhetorics. In 1606 he was among its competitors in the *Landjuweel* at Haarlem. His Baptist parents endowed him with a detestation of the doctrine of original sin and predestination. Baptist beliefs and fundamental Protestantism, however, were at odds with his exuberant zest for life and his deep sense of beauty. He drifted into the camp of the humanists during the fight between the Remonstrants and the Contra-Remonstrants. The intolerance of both groups and their constant religious bickerings caused him to begin once more a spiritual pilgrimage. He looked for stability, beauty, unity, and for something more than the pale negations and even paler assertions of the Libertines. In his own way he was a latitudinarian. He could compose a poetical appeal, for instance, for the Calvinist Walloon orphanage, for he held that the care of unfortunates was the responsibility of all Christians and stood above membership in a single church.

Like Grotius, whom he greatly admired, Vondel began to regard the early Christian Church as ideal, but unlike Grotius he came to consider the Roman Catholic Church as its successor. Vondel's studies of pre-Reformation Amsterdam, his love of its historic buildings and churches, the tragedies in his personal life which became heavier as he grew older, and his reverence and respect for authority and unity carried him in 1642 into the arms of Catholicism. After he embraced Rome, his circle of friends became limited to a few close friends like Tesselschade, who also became a convert. The *Altar-Pieces* he wrote to justify his new faith are as much propaganda as religious expression.

Vondel was fifty-four at the time of his conversion, and some of his most productive years lay before him. His change of faith did not affect the demand for his works or his reception by the town fathers. At eighty-four he translated Ovid's *Metamorphoses* and was busy composing occasional poetry. His last production was an epithalamium for the marriage of his favorite niece, Anna Blok. At the time of that work he was eighty-seven and still trying to provide for his children and grandchildren. He was ninety-one when he died. A few days before his death when he had the shivers, he humorously suggested to his friend and first biographer, Geeraert Brandt (1626–85), that a fitting epitaph might be:

> *Here in peace lies Vondel old:*
> *He died because he was so cold.*

His literary progress like his spiritual one was slow but remarkably consistent. His first work a *Schriftuerlijk Bruylofts Reffereyn* (Writing Referring to Marriage), appeared in 1605 and followed strictly the style of the chamber. Then came a great outpouring of poems and plays, the latter often based on Roman models. *Het Pascha: Ofte de Verlossinghe Israëls uyt Egypten* (The Passover or Israel's Escape out of Egypt) was produced in 1612 by the Brabanter Chamber and shows the path Vondel was later to take. He viewed Israel's flight from bondage as a parallel of Holland's liberation from Spanish oppression. Shortly Vondel moved over to the Eglantier, which staged his *Palamedes*, a tempestuous defense of Oldenbarnevelt and a protest against the Calvinists for stifling the intellectual, religious, and political freedom of the city.

Although the majority of his plays are ordinarily based on classical or Biblical themes, his best known work—and most successful so far as performance is concerned—was the historical drama, *Gysbreght van Aemstel*, which has become a part of the Dutch national heritage. Historically sound and filled with Roman Catholicism though composed before his conversion, Vondel writes in the tradition of Virgil. The play is the epic of Amsterdam wherein according to God's plan Gysbreght assumes the role of an Aeneas and starts Amsterdam on its way to become the first city of the world.

Vondel's poetic and dramatic works show an almost fantastic knowledge of history. They range in subject from Constantine to Mary Stuart, from Adam to the apostles Peter and Paul. He wrote twenty-four original plays in addition to many translations, and after he was over forty the quality of his writing increased tremendously. He modeled his work more and more on Greek authors. It was in his later years that he composed his two greatest plays, *Lucifer* (1653) and *Adam in Ballingschap* (Adam in Exile) (1664).

Lucifer is a Dutch play more discussed than many others outside the Netherlands, for some scholars infer that it was the inspiration for Milton's *Paradise Lost*. Probably Vondel and Milton both based their work on *Adamus Exul* by Grotius. Vondel's *Lucifer* is the story of the revolt of the apostate angels against the throne of Heaven, but

with the Roman Catholic view that Lucifer and his followers were endowed with freedom of the will and thus
capable of both good and evil. Lucifer's position in Heav-
en before his fall was that of stadtholder. As Vondel depicts him he is not all bad. He is essentially of high moral
character and succumbed to the forces of evil until he
reached a point of no return:

> *How have I erred so far from duty's path?*
> *I have adjured my Maker: how can I*
> *Before that Light disguise my blasphemy*
> *And wickedness? Retreat availeth not.*
> *Nay, I have gone too far. What remedy?*
> *What best to do amid this hopelessness?*
> *The time brooks no delay. One moment's time*
> *Is not enough, in time it may be called,*
> *This brevity 'twixt bliss and endless doom.*
> *But 'tis too late. No cleansing for my stain*
> *Is here. All hope is past. What remedy?*
> *Hark! there I hear God's trumpet blow without.*

Adam in Ballingschap, which treats the fall of man,
shows Vondel's interest in dramatic technique and the
profound psychology of his characterization. To the poet
the fall is a "fall from the union of love to the isolation of
selfishness." Adam plans self-destruction. He rants and
raves, and Eve at first reacts angrily. She then is filled with
pity and says, "Wouldst commit mortal sin for my wishes?"
With those words Adam is restored to both his love and
his desire to live. The two face exile together.

At this point in his life, Vondel's form of Renaissance
tragedy has become more personal. His magnificently restrained, but highly flexible, verse soars in these later plays

to heights untouched by other Dutch poets. The figures of speech spring spontaneously from his imagination, and the "vision of his mind's eye" is experienced as a verbal emotion. His sublime mastery of language and poetic diction has the quality of organ music. His verse glides with beauty. "He was the Rubens of Dutch literature, and his art equals the painter's in vastness of range and grandeur of execution." His poetry sang, and a number of his works have been set to music—by a Dutch composer in the seventeenth century and an American one in the twentieth.

Vondel's career spanned the greatest era of the city he loved. His verse calls to mind the times in which he lived, and his lines carved in stone such as those on the entrance to the Begijnhof make his Amsterdam more vital for us today. One can literally make a tour of the city by just stopping at places connected with the poet. Start at the Schrierstoren and walk along the Zeedijk to the Roman Catholic church in the attic and the Oude Kerk. Then continue by the Gulden Wan to the Warmoesstraat where he lived as a child and later carried on the trade of a hose merchant. To the house of his father displaying the signboard *"De Trouw"* Vondel brought his bride. Later he moved to larger quarters on the same street to a house that at one time had the gable stone *"De Kraeck"* but which subsequently became Number 110. Here, under his father's signboard, Vondel carried on the family business. Here he buried his wife and many children. Here he wrote the *Gijsbreght*, the glory piece of Amsterdam.

It is a short walk via the Pijlsteeg to the Dam with the buildings for which he composed poems of dedication. It was on the Dam that he read poems of welcome for distinguished visitors. Leading into the Dam is the Kalverstraat, off which is the entrance to the Begijnhof with the Vondel verses in the walls. Next go to 459 Prinsengracht to the house where Vondel was forced to move because of the extravagance of his son, and then to the Bank van Leening on the O. Z. Voorburgwal, which still stands and where the elderly poet was forced to labor as a porter to support his daughter Anna and three grandchildren by his wastrel son. Follow him to better quarters now, 201 Singel, a pretty house called *"De Witte Molen,"* where he spent his few remaining years.

The older he became, the harsher the vicissitudes of life he endured, the more industriously he worked and the better the results. God was indeed his shepherd. Until he died his imagination soared in fancy to the new lands which the Dutch were colonizing. He rarely left Amsterdam, but by means of travel books, he journeyed in spirit from the quays along which he liked to wander to the White Sea and the Indian Ocean. Not far from the wharves with their cosmopolitan bustle, exotic smells, noises, and many tongues, up the Dam is the Nieuwe Kerk, where Vondel was finally laid to rest. Next door is the City Hall, the symbol of all that the poet loved and revered. A fitting end to the pilgrimage would be to take a tram to Vondel Park on the Stadhouderskade, not far from the Rijksmuseum, which houses the treasures of Rembrandt. One park, one street, one church, one museum of the University of Amsterdam named in his memory. They are mere physical reminders. His name will live as long as survives the Dutch language in which he expressed his genius and his times.

Poetry and music through time immemorial have been linked together. The verses of the poets have been constantly set to music, and the melodies of the musicians have been given lyrics by the poets. Reference has already been made to the influence of poets like Vondel, Bredero, Hooft, and Starter on the popular music of their age. It is unfortunate that the musicians of Amsterdam in the golden age could not achieve the same standards of excellence as did the poets and the painters. Music in Amsterdam in the seventeenth century declined, and the Northern Netherlands during the period had nothing which could compare musically with the output of such South Netherlands composers as Orlandus Lassus in the previous century.

Music suffered at the hands of the Reformation, but it did not disappear. A synod held at Dort in 1574 and another at Edam four years later decreed that all organs had to be removed from the churches. In Amsterdam this was easier said than done because the town magistrates who owned the churches refused to abide by the rulings of the synods. Thus the great organ in the Oude Kerk and others in the city were saved from Protestant vandalism and bigotry. To the ministers the organs were the works of the devil, but the public at large liked them and were not averse to a little flirting with "Old Nick." Organ music might be barred from worship, but at odd intervals they did play secular music and the songs of the psalmists. Eventually the organ returned to the church service, but considerably later at Amsterdam than in some other churches in Holland. It scored one of its initial triumphs at The Hague. Constantijn Huygens, a musician himself, could not endure the singing of psalms by the congregation without musical accompaniment. As he said: "It was more like howling and screeching than singing as if there were merit in outshouting one another and the loudest would carry off the prize." At Leiden through Huygen's efforts the organ was a part of the service by 1640, but it was not until forty years later, October 18, 1680, that this was true in Amsterdam.

What about Amsterdam music then? The Regents hired city organists to play at specified times for the pleasure of the city inhabitants. The most famous of these was the musician and composer, Jan Pietersz. Sweelinck (1562–1621), who performed on the great organ in the Oude Kerk. The magnificent doors of that instrument were done by Maarten van Heemskerk (1498–1574). About the organ in the Nieuwe Kerk an English visitor remarked: "We went into the new great Church, built by the Reform'd, and here is the *biggest Organ* saw and plais so very fine, that you would almost swear there were human voices." Some city organists of note were Dirk Sweelinck, Jacob van Noord, the brothers Willem, Joannes, and Nicholas Lossy, and Willem Aertzen. In 1590 Sweelinck was receiving 300 guilders a year for his services. This was later cut to 100 guilders with an equal amount for housing. Nicholas Lossy in 1645 annually was paid 450 guilders, which was lowered by 150 guilders after a fire stopped performances in the Nieuwe Kerk. The salaries of the organists varied with the church. Ordinarily the organist in the Oude or the Nieuwe Kerk received 150 guilders a year and the organist in the Westerkerk 50 guilders less.

The most outstanding musician of the period was Sweelinck, who, as is so often the case, was not appreciated in his own times. He dedicated many of his songs to wealthy Amsterdam patrons and set to music Latin, French, and Italian poems. So limited was his appeal at home that the four books of psalms that he wrote music for were printed in French rather than Dutch. His instrumental music was copied by his admirers in the upper class, but remained inaccessible to or unwanted by a wider audience. Consequently his manuscripts became scattered, and it was his pupils who eventually brought back some of his works to be performed in Holland. When in the nineteenth century the composer enjoyed a revival, over ten volumes of his work were discovered. All had been preserved by foreign collectors. Not a single Sweelinck composition was found in Holland. With Sweelinck's death there was a decline in Amsterdam of musical composition which was not wholly revived until after the 1890's when Willem Mengelberg took over the leadership of the Amsterdam *Concertgebouw*.

This does not mean there was an end to public performance. There were always the street musicians who then and now give Amsterdam part of its charm. Their numbers were swelled by English performers who sang madrigals. Dramatic music came to the city slowly. In the first part of the century it did not go much beyond the farce and the use of the chorus in drama. As the century progressed, especially between 1643 and 1648, concerts began to be given in a quite different vein. In 1662 the musicians of the King of France gave seven performances at the Schouwburg. The concert had arrived, but ballet and opera lacked sponsors. About 1686 the Regents decided to bring opera to the Schouwburg. Thomas Arendsz. was commissioned with that task and had specific instructions that the opera had to be either Italian, French, or Low German.

The Amsterdamer loved to hear tunes played on the *klokkenspels* which rang out over the city for a quarter of an hour in the early evening and for half an hour during the closing of the city gates and the setting of the city barriers. As the tunes were set mechanically, the master of the *klokkenspels* could plan a number of pieces. There was a *klokkenspel* at the Oude Kerk, the West Church, the South Church, the Regulierstoren, and the new City Hall.

The Regents employed for important occasions a state company of players, who were also open for hire by private groups and individuals. They gave concerts and played for dances. Four of them were given a monopoly to provide the music at all wedding celebrations because performers from foreign countries and other areas in the Netherlands were moving into a province which the city musicians felt belonged solely to them.

The music mostly associated with seventeenth-century Amsterdam is popular music heard in the streets or just inside or outside the tavern doors. On a higher plain it is the sound of strings and voices filling the salons and chambers of the wealthy. Jan Steen, Dirk Hals, C. Nelscher, and a whole host of genre artists depict music lessons or performances within the family or the tavern circle. There was a genuine interest in music on the popular level, and many prominent burghers, poets, and statesmen were accomplished performers.

Music fascinated Vondel. He played the lute and his poetry throbs with beat and melody. To him the art of song "charms the soul out of the body, filling it with rare delight—a foretaste of the bliss of angels." When he was fortunate enough to be invited to Muiden, he was in ecstacy. There Hooft had a considerable number of house concerts. It is not too far fetched to suppose that Constantijn Huygens, who had played before James I of England, could be called upon to perform. The gifted Tesselschade played the guitar, and Hooft's first wife, Christina van Erp, was a talented harpist. Also to Muiden came that famous singer from the South Netherlands, Francisca Duarte, whom Hooft called the "French Nightingale."

There were musical groups besides those at Muiden. Admittedly some such soirées spent more time with flirting, jesting, and drinking than with music. The paintings of the time show this rather vividly. To the contrary, however, is a print published by C. van der Passe which shows a musical evening without extra activities. At one such affair a strict Contra-Remonstrant could not curb his "joy at the zest"; he had a marvelous time at the home of Sweelinck, who played on the harpsicord at least twenty-five variations of the song "The Merry May is now in its Season."

Then there were the music halls, which ranged from brothel fronts to places where one could hear and enjoy good music. A patron could also obtain instruments so that he could join the performers, but if his playing was miserable, he stood to buy beer for the house. Music halls as well as the red-light district flourished throughout Amsterdam in spite of admonitions from the clergy. Establishments where good music could be found were the Huis Lustenburg on the Singel outside the Regulierspoort and the 't Huis te Sinnelust where the Arabic scholar, Jan Theunisz., sold spirits. Another excellent place was the Domus Organica (Organ House) which was operated on the Rokin about 1670 by a Richard Hancock. This establishment had several chambers provided with clave-cimbels, clavichords, cornets, lutes, and viola da gambas. In addition to its musical standards the Organ House also enjoyed a good reputation for its wine, beer, pastries, and oysters. A nightly concert was performed from four to ten.

The age was a music-loving one. A high percentage of the people knew something about music and dancing. Song books such as *The Court of Love* and *The Lover's Song Book* were in the hands of most of the young people —and some older ones—and made their appearance at parties. Traditional songs were set to old tunes or to the newer foreign ones coming in from England, France, and Italy. Some old tunes acquired new lyrics from the hands of Bredero, Hooft, Vondel, Starter, and a host of lesser lights. The presses of Jan Evertsz., Paulus Aertsz., Dirck Pietersz. Voscuyl, Paulus Mallhysz., not to mention the Blaeus and Elzeviers, published songs for every taste and every occasion. The most significant Amsterdam music publisher was Estienne Rogers, who came to the city some years after the death of Rembrandt.

Amsterdam fell heir to Antwerp in the manufacturing of musical instruments. Its claviers and klokkenspels were well known, but the market was heaviest in violins. Well known violin-makers were Johannes Bouwmeester, Gerrit Menslage, Philip del Mot, and Cornelis Cleymen. Next in significance were the cither-makers such as Pieter Frans Borsch, Jan Boudwijn, and others. Amsterdam also manufactured drums and brasses, and what musical instruments were not made in the city could be easily found in Amsterdam music shops. As one English traveler commented, the Dutch taught the English how to make musical instruments and the "Laying on Colours in Oyl." It is in this latter category that the artistic genius of Amsterdam is best known to posterity.

Painting in Amsterdam like architecture not only survived the Alteratie and the ravages of war but also the loss of church patronage so important to builder, sculptor, and painter during the Renaissance. This persistence indicates two things: first there were well established schools and traditions of painting in Holland before the decline of the South Netherlands and second that the Calvinist Church was unable to eradicate painting any more than it was able to close the stage. It is well to remember that at the time that Amsterdam painting was at its height, the English Puritans added "a love of painting" to the charges against Charles I.

Carel van Mander, biographer of Netherlandish painters, is sketchy about Amsterdam painting in the sixteenth century. He does say that the first artist of note working in the city was Jacob Cornelisz. van Oostsanen, but he fails to mention Cornelis Anthonisz., who among other things did the earliest extant map of the Netherlands. By 1570 in Amsterdam a boom in painting was already under way, and a goodly number of artists living in the vicinity of the present Waag were providing a new aspect to the city's cultural life. Nine years later the painters, sculptors, and engravers separated from their brick-laying brothers in the Lieve Vrouwegilde and formed an Amsterdam chapter of the St. Lucas Guild. In their new freedom, the members of the St. Lucas Guild became more and more associated with the chambers of rhetorics and with the traditions of painting in the South Netherlands. Soon the guild would receive into its hall refugee brothers from Brabant and Flanders. The old Holland traditions would merge into the Dutch school. The South pressed art towards one attitude of mind while the "North inherited the Netherlands in the full wealth of their variety." Jan van Hout, who was in Amsterdam between 1585 and 1587, did an altar piece for the Agnietenklooster while Van Oostsanen, who was under the influence of Flemish and Italian artists, did altar pieces such as "The Gift of the Magi" (school of Roger van den Weyden), "The Birth of Christ," and "Saul and the Witches of Endor."

Loss of ecclesiastical patronage was compensated by the popularity of art, not only in Amsterdam, but in cities throughout Holland—an area which did not have a million people but whose artistic achievements became world famous. Dutch painting was the glory of the golden age of Holland, and the people patronized the artist. The rooms of inns, the banquet halls of *schutterij*, operating rooms in hospitals, guildhalls, board rooms of charitable institutions, hospitals, orphanages, leperhouses, homes for the aged, and public and semi-public buildings were all hung with paintings, usually single or group portraits. An English traveler was amazed that almshouses and houses of correction boasted paintings, and that "Butchers, Cobblers, and meanist People, have a great many, and of the sort pretty good and well set out." Small wonder the picture-stalls at the fairs flourished, and foreigners such as the diarist, John Evelyn, came to them to purchase paintings and "drolleries." Not only were herring and spices shipped out from the Amsterdam quays, but fish were also featured in the many still-lifes that were exported.

Amsterdam was the focal point for North Netherlandish art. The reasons for the city's position are simple. There was no city in Holland that expended as much money for public charities as Amsterdam. There was no other city in which the *schutterij* played a greater role. Furthermore Amsterdam contained the richest commercial community in the world. Burghers became patrons of the arts and decorated their homes with paintings. The city also employed well-known artists and engravers to embellish public buildings and to commemorate special anniversaries and historical events.

Although Amsterdam was the magnet for artists and the center of the art trade in the United Provinces, just a small number of the truly great Dutch artists were born within the city walls. One must note that these men did not come to Amsterdam from small hamlets and rustic villages, but from cities that already had an active art tradition and where the St. Lucas Guilds and painting flourished. Rembrandt and Metsu came from Leiden, Ruisdael and Van der Helst from Haarlem, Bol and Maes from Dordrecht, Gérard Lairesse from Luik, Pieter de Hoogh, Emanuel de Witte, and Simon de Vlieger from Delft and Rotterdam. One could expand the list considerably. These artists came to the city in person (*naar den vleesche*) and remained there, often until their deaths. Some of them came searching for a place where they might enjoy a career. Others came as mere youths, like Rembrandt, looking for instruction. Suffice to say there were nearly a thousand artists active in Amsterdam during the seventeenth century.

It is impossible to discuss even a fraction of the artists and their works without doing injustice to men and paintings. Many of them were prolific. Rembrandt executed 650 paintings, 300 etchings, and over 2,000 drawings. There is a complete literature on him as there is on other of the great artists of his day. One approach to an understanding of the more salient features of Amsterdam art during the period is to consider it according to subject matter, though admittedly the device is clumsy. The artists customarily worked in all areas, but will be considered mainly in the area in which they excelled.

All if possible did portrait and group commissions, for they supplied the artist with his chief source of income. Such paintings abound. The wealthy wanted to be immortalized on canvas, and the lesser folk who could afford it had similar ambitions. Among the forerunners of the period was Dirck Jacobsz. (*c.* 1495–1567), who did a rather good portrait of Anna Occo, and a *schutterij* piece (a group portrait of a military guild such as Rembrandt's "Night Watch") which had all the animation and composition of a high-school class picture taken in early twentieth-century America. Cornelisz. Anthonisz. (1500-1553) painted Reymont III, a councilor of Charles V. Of more significance is his *"Braspennigsmaal Tijd"* (1553), which shows a banquet of the *schutterij* of St. Joris Voetboogdoelen, and which is the first of a long series of Dutch pieces showing the *schutterij* at table. Dirck Barentsz. (1534–92) has a magnificent panel, the *"Pos-eters"* (1566), which shows the Kloveniers Guild eating a traditional dish. Peter Aertsen (1508–73) did portraits and also "The Gift of the Magi," which is more Italianate than Van Oostsanen's treatment of the same theme because there is a better use of light and closer attention to detail.

Of greater worth was Cornelis Ketel (1548–1616), a traditional figure who did not parrot the Italians, but did know the Italian style. His best portrait is of Maria Claes Gaeff. Ketel's engravings are worthy of note, but his *"Het corporaalschap van Kapitein Dirck Jacobsz. Rosecrans en Luitenant Pauw 1588"* is of more importance because it shows a *schutterij* company involved in a common action.

Ketel closed out the sixteenth century in Amsterdam art
along with Gillis van Coninixloo (1545–1606), a Fleming
who had spent a number of years in Amsterdam and died
there. Coninixloo, a transitional figure between Flemish
and Dutch painting, attracted to his studio at Amsterdam
a goodly number of young men, the best being Hercules
Seghers (1589–1640?). Nicholas Elias, who was born in
Amsterdam 1590/1 and lived there until his death between
1650 and 1656, did more Regent and *Schutterij* pieces than
any other Amsterdam artist. His works in composition and
color rank with those of the Haarlemer, Frans Hals. His
last important work, "The Regents of the Walloon Orphanage," is his masterpiece and compares favorably with
the best. It shows the influence of Rembrandt, and it is
similar to an early work of Bartholomeus van der Helst
(1613–70). Thomas de Keyser (1596/7–1667) was at least
as good a portrait painter as Elias. De Keyser's grey backgrounds remind one of the backgrounds found in Rembrandt's earlier paintings.

Historical paintings were very much in vogue. They
could refer to passing contemporary events, be portrait
pieces for a guildhall, or be based on Biblical, classical,
mythological, or allegorical themes. Pieter Lastman (1583–
1633), Rembrandt's teacher, used mainly Biblical subjects
and like a goodly number of North Netherlands writers
and painters expected that all good things originated in
Italy. Lastman had visited Italy in the springtime of Caravaggio, whose glaring light effects and chiaroscuro were
carried to far greater heights by Rembrandt. Lastman's
preoccupation with Biblical scenes may have had some
influence on his churlish student from Leiden.

Another "Italian" was Jan Symonsz. Pynas (1583–1631),

who had been deeply influenced by Adam Elsharmer of Verona. Pynas' works during his lifetime were in great demand, but they are extremely spotty. Perhaps his poorest painting is "Christ on the Cross," at present in the Mauritshuis at The Hague. The best painter of Biblical scenes—Rembrandt excepted—was Cornelisz. Moeyaert (c. 1600–c. 1657). His composition is excellent and his drawing forceful. His best canvas is probably "Abraham's vision in the Land of Canaan." He also painted some masterly Regent pieces.

The surgeons perhaps more than any other group wanted to be remembered by posterity. Aert Pietersz. (1550–1612) painted an "Anatomy Lesson by Dr. Egberts" (1603) in which he grouped twenty-nine people. De Keyser in 1619 painted another lesson by the same teacher with only the lecturer and five observers. Nicholas Elias in 1625 did an anatomy lesson, but the most famous one was completed in 1632 by young Rembrandt van Rijn—"The Anatomy Lesson of Dr. Tulp," which almost overnight made the young artist famous. Later in life he did the "Anatomy Lesson of Dr. Deyman." Rembrandt of course was magnificent in all areas and consequently will be treated separately.

Rembrandt had a number of students and followers who quite often changed with the times and pursued current trends, especially after the master began more and more to follow his own lonely path. Many of these students became world famous in their own right. Space does not permit a full discussion of Rembrandt's students, who throughout most of their lives were associated with Amsterdam. Carel Fabritus (1620–54) died young, but might have had more potential than any other of Rembrandt's pupils. Ferdinand Bol's (1616–80) best effort is the "Regents of the Lepers' House," which shows a strong Rembrandt influence. At present this hangs in the Burgomaster's Chamber of the City Hall. Govert Flinck (1615–60) toward the end of Rembrandt's life was much more popular than his master. He moved over to Van Dyck's technique in portraiture, did one of the panels in the new City Hall, and was considered by Vondel to be Amsterdam's finest artist. Flinck died leaving behind a valuable collection of paintings, many by the hand of his old teacher.

Nicholas Maes (1632–93) came to Rembrandt from Dort. He was a strong colorist, but later in his life his paintings became slippery and cold. His work became increasingly mundane as he concentrated on portraits of the hyper-elegant Heeren and their wives who were setting the standards of late seventeenth-century Amsterdam. His outstanding work, "Het Gebed zonder Einde" (Our Daily Bread), shows an old woman sitting and offering her thankful blessing for the meager meal of which she is about to partake. Its theme, its composition, its color, and its dramatic treatment make this one of the true masterpieces of Dutch art.

Another disciple of Rembrandt was Bartholomeus van der Helst, who was born in Haarlem in 1613, came to Amsterdam as a child, and died there in 1670. His Regent pieces and *schutterij* pieces approach those of Rembrandt. He was a portrait painter par excellence. He lacks Rembrandt's emotion. Van der Helst clothed his people in bright hues, and even in his large group arrangements, the individuals do not lose their identities. His best *schutterij* pieces compare favorably with the "Night Watch." His art was good and his patrons were satisfied.

The most influential Amsterdam painter in the last part of the seventeenth century was Gérard de Lairesse, a Fleming who came to Amsterdam in 1667. He was very much under the influence of the French baroque, and he had many followers in his adopted city. His "Seleucus and Stratonice" is well done and its lighting is excellent. At the time De Lairesse was under Rembrandt's influence. More exemplary of his style is *"Huldinging van Flora."* It is classical in theme and loaded with cherubs and other extraneous materials so dear to the French art of the period.

Amsterdam produced some of the finest Dutch landscape painters. The first artist of note in that area was Conincxloo, who had a considerable number of followers. Hendrich Avercamp (1585–after 1663) worked in Amsterdam and his winter scenes and those of skaters on the canals are known to all lovers of Dutch art. Jan van de Capelle (1625–79) and David Vinckboons (1578–1629) also did Dutch winter scenes.

Other landscape painters of note were Hercules Seghers, Jacob Ruysdael (1628–82), and Meindert Hobbema (1638–1709). These last two and their paintings are well known to the art world and they were quite significant as influences on the work of the English painters Constable and Turner. Paulus Potter (1625–54) and his farm animals, Anthonie van Borssom, Adriaen van der Velde, and Philips Koninck (1619–88) are landscape artists whose works are in most of the large museums of the United States and Europe. Ruysdael did delightful seascapes, but perhaps the best known seascape is the "Beach at Scheveningen" (1643) by Simon de Vlieger (1601–52). The most unique "Dauber" of ships and seamen was William van der Velde the elder (1611/12–93), who in 1666 from a small boat in line of fire sketched a naval battle between England and the Netherlands. So impressed was Charles II by his daring that he invited him to London as a Royal painter, where he remained until his death a good many years later. His sons Adriaen and William the Younger were famous for both land and seascapes.

The Dutch and Amsterdam artists discovered beauty in the home and painted subjects that more highly sophisticated critics such as Horace Walpole did not consider proper for art. In our own time Sacheverell Sitwell complains that Dutch artists with the exception of Rembrandt set out to narrate or describe but not to create. There is a germ of truth to this, and the majority of Dutch artists were limited as compared to Rembrandt. This would be true of most artists of any age. The Dutch artists did turn to subjects they enjoyed and often with an extraordinary sense of realism imparted a certain individuality into the still life, the landscape, or the simple scene they depicted. To ignore the intimate relationship between the artist and his work is to be blind to imagination. To be overly concerned about the subject matter of art is often to be boorish or snobbish.

The Dutch genre painters were realists. Often poorly educated except in their craft, they looked at life around them and depicted it as they saw and felt it. They were in the tradition of Breughel, but they took that tradition and gave it their own interpretation. David Vinckboons was a close follower of Breughel as was Peter Codde (1599–1678). Amsterdam had no Jan Steen or Adriaen van Ostade, but it did have Adriaen Brouwer (1605/6–39) who spent some time in the city. His paintings of card-playing farmers, sleeping youths, drunken farmers in a field, a smoker, and primitive interiors show the seamy aspects of Dutch life. William Duijester (1599–1635) and Gabriel Metsu (1630–67) depicted dance parties, visits from neighbors, and scenes portraying upper-class drinking and courting which are in marked contrast to Brouwer and to Pieter Quast (1605/6–47), whose riffraff is not quite so earthy and crude as is Brouwers. Simon Kick (1603–52) and Emanuel de Witte (1617–92) have their viewers peek into stately interiors while Pieter de Hoogh (1629–77) takes them into Dutch homes with colorful tiles and fireplaces or out into peaceful courtyards to enjoy with a neighbor a friendly cordial and lively conversation.

William van Aerlst, Walter Kalff, and Melchoir de Hondécoter along with Jan Baptist Weenick were among the Amsterdam artists who painted excellent still lifes. From them we get insights into the everyday things of Amsterdam living: plates of bread, fish or fruit, dressed and undressed game, poultry, old glass, Delftware, etc. The better known painters of flowers were Van Aelst and Jan van Huysum. When looking at a Van Aelst work, Samuel Pepys had to touch a drop of moisture on one of the flowers to assure himself that it was not real. The most outstanding artist treating flowers was Rachael Ruysch (1665–1750). Her craft was so great that the viewer forgets he is looking at a painting of a floral arrangement and has the impression that he is looking into nature itself. Ruysch has a real strength to her strokes and avoids the pitfalls of many painters whose flowers are too pretty and too delicate to be real. She along with Judith Leyster, who spent some time in Amsterdam, were two superior woman artists who could compete in their somewhat narrow spheres with the male painters.

Most of the artists were underpaid, extravagant, and drank up a large percentage of their money. Later in life many died in abject poverty or were forced to take other employment to supplement their meager or nonexistent income from art. In addition to finding menial jobs, some became illustrators of maps and books. Others committed their best works to etchings and engravings. Rembrandt in his leaner years helped support himself in this manner. There were at least eighty-five well-known etchers and engravers in seventeenth-century Amsterdam. Counting the unknown professionals and the amateurs the number must have been legion as it was in the case of the painters. The flourishing trade in printing and cartography created a demand for etchers and engravers. So well-advanced and renowned were the Dutch in these areas that the English called the mordant used in etching a "Dutch Bath."

The Amsterdam market offered four types of prints: woodcuts, engraving, etchings, and what the Dutch called "black art" (*zwarte kunst*). This last is mezzotinting, which was developed in Holland by Prince Rupert of the Palatinate when he was a young man living in Holland. The woodcut goes back into the art of the Middle Ages, and after 1550 its vitality was on the wane. The first Amsterdam woodcutter of note was Jacob Oostsanen. Dry point engravings also began to appear in the Middle Ages, but unlike woodcuts they continued to be used extensively in book illustrations throughout the seventeenth and eighteenth centuries. Etching was born at the beginning of the sixteenth century, developed in the seventeenth century, and reached its highest state of perfection under the needle of Rembrandt. Mezzotinting, although making its debut in the seventeenth century, did not become the vogue until later.

Among the Amsterdam etchers of landscapes were Jac. Savery and David Vinckboons. Both were very Flemish in their approach. Next to Rembrandt the most outstanding master of the etching needle was Hercules Seghers. "Het Landscap met de puntige Rots" (The Landscape with the pointed Rocks) is one of his best. In it he portrays a highly melancholic Amsterdam scene filled with fantasy. The entire view is nearly dreamlike, and his use of wave lines—his famous nervous technique—makes the work one of the finest etched landscapes. During his life, Seghers did forty landscapes, twelve ruins or buildings under construction, two still lifes, and four figures. Jacob Ruysdael did twelve etchings, the most famous being "The Tree Oaks" (1649). Reiner Noons (c. 1623–67), who called himself "Zeeman," did 166 prints. Adriaen van de Velde, Jan van Capelle, among a whole host of others, also did Dutch landscapes. Karel de Jardin and Claes Moeyaert led the group in Amsterdam who used the needle to depict Italian scenes.

Among the engravers of genre scenes was Pieter Serwouter (1591–1650), whose best effort was "The Inn of the Beggars," after a painting by Vinckboons. He was also a book illustrator of note. Claes Jansz. Visscher (1587–1652) did stately interiors showing upper-class families in their milieu. His *"Het Gebed voor den Maaltijd"* (Grace) has magnificent detail from a small crib in the dining room to the carvings around the leaded casement windows.

There were also the portrait engravers and the book

illustrators. Such was Michiel le Blon (1587–1656), who spent much of his life in Amsterdam. He illustrated Bredero's song book and a number of emblem books. Cornelis Danckerts, his two sons, and his two grandsons were all engravers and collectively they spanned the seventeenth century. Crispijn de Passe (1595–1670) had a following in his day as did Romeijn de Hooghe (1645–1708), whose historical scenes such as "The Arrival of William III at the Hague" and "The Battle of Naarden" were very much in vogue. The best of Dutch engraving as was true in painting came to an end with Gérard de Lairesse. His "Rape of Proserpine" is highly indicative of the elegant classicism which was the style of the time. Lairesse was tremendously productive, and many of his prints especially the earlier ones, have an unusual freshness and a beauty.

The maps of the time were often works of art. Paintings by Vermeer and other artists often show Dutch interiors with highly illustrated maps hung on the walls. The maps of the time were often loaded with dolphins, fish, mermaids, natives, and highly decorative cartouches which made the maps and the atlases of Hondius, Jansson, and the Bleaus as decorative as they were useful. In addition, city maps were often drawn showing all the buildings, such as the map of Amsterdam by Pieter Bast in 1597 or a later one done by J. de Ram in about 1681.

In a class by himself, contributing to Amsterdam art but going his own way, towered Rembrandt—Amsterdam's and Holland's greatest etcher and painter. There have been few artists in any age and in any city whose artistic scope was as wide and as varied as life itself. His self-portraits show the bloom and the gradual decay of a man and of Man. In his portraits, be it "The Jewish Bride,"

"Saskia," or his son "Titus," the subjects take on an air of individuality as they appeared to the searching eye of the artist. In his historical paintings he used the event to show the universality of man's problems and the weaknesses of his character. "The Prodigal Son" is such that one wonders if Rembrandt, filled with guilt feelings, was not painting himself. He could take what was good in chiaroscuro and carry it to boundaries undreamed of by Caravaggio. All that one has to do is to compare Rembrandt's "Christ at Emmaus" with one done on a similar theme by the Italian master. His most discussed painting, *"Het Korporaalschap van Kapitein Banning Cocq,"* called "The Night Watch" is like no other *schutterij* piece. In it Rembrandt played with light and shade making a dramatic whole of the composition which is breath-taking.

After he painted "The Night Watch," Rembrandt's fortunes took a turn for the worse. His wife Saskia died. His extravagance forced him into bankruptcy, and his house and valuable art collection were auctioned off for a small percentage of their actual worth. To prevent his future earnings from being seized by creditors, he became an employee of his mistress, Hendrickje Stoffels, and his son Titus, whose fortune he had wasted. His style was turning farther and farther away from the tastes of his time, but he was neither rejected by society nor forced to grovel in abject poverty. He still received good commissions, but not so many, and his house on the Rosengracht was a large and comfortable dwelling according to the current standards. He continued to collect art treasures, but on a much more limited scale. When he died he left Cornelia, his daughter by Hendrickje Stoffels, a considerable legacy. But he was plagued with money problems, partly a result of his own extravagance and his passion for collecting. As he grew older, he became more difficult. It was more a case of his rejecting Amsterdam than of Amsterdam rejecting him. He was his own worst enemy, and at times appears to have enjoyed the role.

After personal sadness and bankruptcy, he showed a greater maturity in his work. His religious subjects became movingly uncomplicated with warmer colors and superb lighting. His brush strokes became broader and more spontaneous until in his last years they seem to have been applied with a palette-knife rather than with a brush. In all his life he was wholly engrossed with the human element both in himself and the people around him. He had a deep concern for man's trials and tribulations and his continual suffering. Like Seghers he painted his landscapes as expressions of his inner life, "but in his etchings and drawings he rendered the surroundings of Amsterdam with tender fidelity." His most important works came out of his inward suffering and were accomplished after he was forty-two.

His pencil and his etching needle portrayed the simple people he met on Amsterdam's streets—mostly the poor, the stranger, the weary, and the confused. The simplicity of his people carried over into the simplicity of his magnificent landscapes. He also did portrait engravings of Saskia, his wealthy friends and his poor ones, and of course himself. Many of his Biblical scenes in black and white are nearly as breath-taking as his paintings. His most famous and surely the most dramatic is "Ecco Homo," which shows Pilate presenting Jesus to the Jewish people.

In his etchings and in his paintings and especially in his drawings, one can see many aspects of the Amsterdam in which he worked and the people he knew, sympathized with, and loved. The same reflection of the city can be found in many other Amsterdam artists who put their impressions of the city on canvas, paper, or panel. That Amsterdam is past, but the greatness of the city culturally and economically still lives. History has been kind to the old sections of Amsterdam. The churches that Rembrandt knew, the houses in which he and many of his friends and enemies lived, the canals, and even some of the bustle of the market place found in the open stalls on the Waterloo Plein and elsewhere are still there. His paintings have been preserved in great numbers by his native city as have those of other Amsterdam artists of his era. Organ recitals are still given in the Oude Kerk, and sailors and visitors still browse through the narrow streets. Traveling musicians and merchants abound. The burghers still patronize inns which functioned when Rembrandt was quenching his thirst, and the red-light district in which he wenched as a young man is still in business. At the right season one can catch a performance of Vondel's *Gijsbrecht* at the Schouwburg. To be sure, neither Rembrandt nor Vondel would feel completely at home in modern Amsterdam. Rembrandt Plein and Vondel Park would be real surprises. Yet there would be a goodly number of recognizable landmarks going back to when Amsterdam was the world's leading center of civilization, back to when Rembrandt came home with joyous excitement from the art stalls to his Saskia in the house on the Joodenbreestraat, back to when Vondel with his head stuffed with verse ambled along the Warmoesstraat after an evening of song and poetry with Tesselschade at Roemer Visscher's house, back to when the two on a given evening if the wind was right could hear rising over the moon-drenched canals and gabled buildings the soaring majesty of Sweelinck's organ.

Selected Readings

Barbour, Violet. *Capitalism in Amsterdam in the 17th Century*. Baltimore, Johns Hopkins Press, 1950.

Barnouw, Adriaan J. *Coming After: an Anthology of Poetry from the Low Countries*. New Brunswick, Rutgers University Press, 1948.

———. *The Dutch: A Portrait Study of the People of Holland*. New York, Columbia University Press, 1940.

———. *Vondel*. New York and London, Scribner's and Sons, 1925.

Blok, Petrus J. *History of the People of the Netherlands*. 5 vols. New York and London, G. P. Putnam's Sons, 1898–1912.

Bloom, Herbert Ivan. *The Economic Activities of the Jews in Amsterdam in the Seventeenth and Eighteenth Centuries*. Williamsport, Pa., The Bayard Press, 1937.

Bredius, A., and H. Brugmans, *et al. Amsterdam in de Zeventiende Eeuw*. 3 vols. 's-Gravenhage, W. P. van Stockum en zoon, 1897–1904.

Selected Readings

Boxer, Charles R. *The Dutch Seaborne Empire, 1600–1800.* New York, Alfred Knopf, 1965.

Brugmans, Hajo. *Opkomst en Bloei van Amsterdam.* Amsterdam, Meulenhoff, 1911.

Carter, Alice. *The English Reformed Church in Amsterdam.* Amsterdam, Scheltema and Holkema, 1964.

D'Ailly, Antoine E., *et al. Zeven Eeuwen Amsterdam.* 6 vols. Amsterdam, Scheltema and Holkema, 1946–51.

Elias, Johan E. *De Vroedschap van Amsterdam, 1578–1795.* 2 vols. Haarlem, V. Loosjes, 1903–1905.

Fremantle, Katharine. *The Baroque Town Hall of Amsterdam.* Utrecht, Haentjen, Dekker en Gumbert, 1959.

Geyl, Pieter. *The Netherlands Divided (1609–1648).* London, Williams and Norgate, Ltd., 1936.

———. *The Netherlands in the Seventeenth Century.* 2 vols. London, Ernest Benn, 1961–64.

———. *The Revolt of the Netherlands (1555–1609).* London, Williams and Norgate, Ltd., 1932.

Guiccardini, Lodovico. *Description of the Low Countries.* London, 1593.

Landheer, Bartholomeus Landheer, ed. *The Netherlands.* Berkeley and Los Angeles, University of California Press, 1943.

Wagenaar, Jan. *Amsterdam, in Zijne Opkomst, Aanwas, Geschiedenissen, Voorregten, Koophandel, Gebouwen, Kerkenstraat, Schoolen, Schutterije, Gilden en Regeeringen.* Amsterdam, I. Tiron, 1765.

Index

A. B. (daughter of Burgomaster Boelens?) : 130

Aboat, Izaak: 106

Academy of Sciences (of Paris) : 109

Accijnhuis: 19

Admiralty Colleges: 38

Admiralty of Amsterdam: 24, 53, 75–76; buildings of, 19; fees of, 75–76

Advocate: 22, 40

Aemstel, Gijsbrecht van: 96, 149

Aeneas: 149

Aerlst, William van: 168

Aertsen, Pieter: 162

Aertsz., Paulus: 158

Aertzen, Willem: 154

African trade: 65, 68, 83

Agnietenklooster, altar piece of: 160

Ainsworth, Henry: 97–98

Albertcuypstraat, markets of: 76

Alteratie: 20, 27, 91, 96, 120, 137, 159

America: 162

Amstel (river) : 5–7, 13; course of, 5, 7, 13; warehouses on, 74

Amsterdam: description and history of, 3ff.; city hall, 4, 8, 19, 20, 22, 24, 27, 44–45, 47, 59, 86, 146, 152, 156, 165; trade and shipping, 6, 36, 50–53, 58, 62–66, 68–69, 74–76, 82, 90; boundaries of, 7, 12; population of, 10; social classes in, 16–17, 44, 47, 78, 92; government of, 20ff., 38, 46; religious policies of, 24ff.; political power of, 26ff.; opposition to Oldenbarnevelt, 27–28, 30–32; Arminian controversy, 28ff.; opposition to House of Orange, 32–33, 37, 39, 41, 43; Spanish policy, 35; siege of, 39; French war, 43; decline of, 44; Descartes on, 45; commercial policies of, 48–49, 59, 61, 84ff.; streets of, 80–81; arts in, 90–91, 109, 117, 160ff.; education in, 92–95, 97; Latin School of, 96; library of, 98; printing in, 83–84, 109–11; university of, 103–105, 152; literature of, 120–21, 125–26, 129; chambers of rhetorics of, 121–

178

23; theater of, 124–26; Hooft and, 131ff.; painting in, 136, 158ff.; Bredero and, 137–39, 141–42, 144–45; Vondel sites of, 151; music in, 153ff.; *Concert-gebouw* of, 155; artists in, 161ff.; reflected by paintings, 168; treatment of Rembrandt, 172–73; historical preservation of, 174–75

Anabaptists: 95–96, 99, 147

Anglo-Dutch wars: 41–42

Anthias, Joseph: 110

Anthonisz., Cornelis: 159, 162

Antwerp: 37, 53, 59, 91, 95, 123, 126, 158; trade and commerce of, 35ff., 50–51, 84; compared with Amsterdam, 37; printing in, 110

Arabic studies: 99

Archangel: 63, 75

Arendsz., Thomas: 155

Armenians: 11

Arminian controversy: 28ff.; pamphlet warfare of, 30–33; *see also* Remonstrants

Arminius, Jacob: 28

Arctic: 52

Athenaeum Illustre: 102, 104, 111

Athias, Joseph: 98

Avercamp, Hendrich: 166

Badens, Francesco: 139

Baeck, Laurens: 131

Bakker, Meeuwes: 6

Baltic, the: 36, 38, 41, 49, 51, 62–63, 65; trade to, 49, 64, 74

Banco de Rialto: 84

Bank van Leening: 53, 86, 152; commission for, 21; financial policies of, 88–90

Bankruptcy Commission: 21

Banks: 19, 53, 86; *see also* Bank van Leening and Exchange Bank

Bantam: 68

Baptists: *see* Anabaptists

Barbary pirates: 65

Barbour, Violet: 56, 58, 86

Barents, Willem: 66–67, 116

Barentsz., Dirck: 162

Barlaeus, Caspar van: 102–103, 113, 120–21, 125, 131

Barnouw, Adriaan J.: 133, 144

Barrowists: 11

Bartjens, Willem: 94–95, 100

Bast, Pieter: 7, 171

Baudartius, Willem: 31

Beemster: 46, 81

Begijnhof: 11, 151–52

Benveniste, Emanuel: 98

Berg, Adriana van der: 124

Besche, Willem de: 64

Beuningen, Conrad van: 42

Beurs: 59, 87; *see also* Exchange Bank

Bicker, Andries: 26–27, 32, 34–40, 63

Bicker, Cornelis: 34, 39–40, 72

Bicker family: 38, 40, 64

Bicker, Jacob: 34, 36

Bicker, Jan: 34, 40

Bicker League: 35, 39, 72

Bicker, Wendela: *see* De Witt

Bie, Cornelius de: 7

Billingsgate: 8

Black Sea: 53

Bleau family: 92, 111–12, 158

Bleau, Joan: 113–14

Bleau, Willem Jansz.: 81, 94, 96, 112–15, 171

Bloemgracht: 113

Blok, Anna: 148

Blommaert, Samuel: 73

Blon, Michiel de: 171

Boelens (burgomaster) : 130
Boerhave, Dr. Herman: 109
Bol, Ferdinand: 161, 165
Bonaparte family: 47
Bontemantel, Hans: 18
Book making and selling: 83–84
Boreel, Adam: 105
Borsch, Pieter Frans: 158
Borssom, Anthonie van: 166
Boudwijn, Jan: 158
Bourse: 53; *see also* exchange
Bouwmeester, Johannes: 158
Boxer, Charles: 72
Brabant and Brabanters: 50, 72, 95, 159
Brahe, Tycho: 113
Brandt, Geraert: 25, 148
Brazil: 58, 72
Breda: 41
Bredero, Gerbrand Adriaensz.: 100, 118, 123ff., 131, 136–37, 153, 158, 171; *schutterij* comments on, 23; attacks on Calvinists, 32; use of Dutch language, 127; dramatic writings of, 138–42; education of, 138; poetry of, 141–44
Breero: *see* Bredero
Brereton, Sir William: 25ff., 57
Breughel, Pieter the Elder: 167
Brink, Bakhuizen van den: 146
Brosterhuysen, John van: 131
Brothels: 9
Broughton, Hugh: 98–99
Brouwer, Adriaen: 168
Brouwersgracht: 74
Brownists: 97–98
Brugsmans, Professor: 146
Bueno, Ephriam: 99
Burgersdijk, Franco: 106
Burgh, Jacob van der: 131
Burgher rights (*poorterschap*) : 78

Burgherweeshuis (orphanage) : 78; *see also* city officials
Burgomasters: powers of, 21–22, 24, 78; selection of, 22, 42; religious policies of, 24ff.

Calvinists: 11, 27ff., 54, 83, 101; divines of, 8; in control of Amsterdam, 32; struggle with Prince Frederick Henry, 32; attitudes on the arts, 123, 159; *see also* Contra-Remonstrants *and* Reformed Church
Cambridge, university of: 97, 103
Campen, Jacob van: 14, 20
Canals: 4–5, 12–13, 83
Cape of Good Hope: 53, 67
Cape Horn: 53
Cape Verde islands: 66
Capelle, Jan van de: 166, 170
Caravaggio, Michelangelo da: 163, 172
Cardinael, Sybrandt Hansz.: 101
Carel, Jan Jansz.: 83
Carlyle, Thomas: 53
Cartography: 159
Catholics: *see* Roman Catholics
Cats, Jacob: 125–26
Central railroad station: 60
Chamber of Assurance: 53
Chambers of rhetorics: 121, 123, 126, 147–48, 159; *Eglantier*, 121, 123, 125, 137–38, 149; *'t Wit Lavender*, 121; Calvinists on, 123; *Landjuweel*, 123, 147
Charles I of England: 159
Charles V, Emperor: 135, 162
Child, Josiah: 62, 88
Chizkoeni (Jewish scholar) : 98
Christenius, Joannes: 102
Christian of Brunswick: 65
Christina, Queen of Sweden: 120

Index

Churches and chapels: 19
City Council: 21 ff., 30
Claeszoon, Cornelis: 110
Clerc, Jean le: 91, 105, 115
Cleymen, Cornelis: 158
Cloth Guild: 79
Codde, Peter: 167
Coffee houses: 8
Colbert, Jean Baptiste: 48, 58
College of Auditors: 21
College of Domestic Squabbles: 21
College of the Masters of Justice: 22
College of Medicine: 104
College of Petty Affairs: 21
College of Surgeons: 104
Collegiants: 106; orphanage of, 93
Cologne publishers: 114
"Compagnie van Verre": 68
Coninixloo, Gillis van: 163, 166
Constable, John: 166
Constantine (Roman Emperor): 96, 146
Contra-Remonstrants: 28ff., 127, 141, 147, 157; in the West India Company, 72; attitude on arts, 118; see also Calvinists
Coornhert, Dirk: 29, 120
Coq, Dr. Frans Banning: 23, 40
Coster, Dr. Samuel: 100–102, 118, 123–24, 131, 138, 141; attack on Calvinists, 32; Academy of, 99, 102, 123, 125–27, 129
Council of Amsterdam: 29
Council of the States General: 103
Court of Holland: 103
Court life and literature: 120
Cromwell, Oliver: 41
Curcellaeus, Stephanus: 105

Dam: see Damrak
Damrak: 7, 10, 59ff., 110, 112, 151–52; description of, 8
Danby: see Osborne
Danckertsz., Cornelis: 12, 171
Danish Sound: 37, 63; Dues, 36–37
Danzig: 63
Deacons' Orphanage: 93
Decker, Jeremias de: 60
Defoe, Daniel: 50
Delaware: 51
Delft: 80, 161
Denmark: 36, 57, 65
Descartes, René: 91, 106–107, 112; on Amsterdam, 45
Deutz. (widow in business): 55
Devonshire, Duke of: 110
Deyman, Dr. Joannes: 104–105, 164
Dijk, Christoffel van: 112
Dijkstraat: 11
Dikes: 7
Dillen, J. G. van: 85
Donne, John: 126
Doorluchtig Gymnasium: see Athenaeum Illustre
Dordrecht: 161, 165; synod at, 101–102, 153
Dort: see Dordrecht
Doublet, George Rataller: 131
Drama, classical themes: 123
Drapers: 10
Drebbel, Cornelis: 120
Drost of Muiden: see Hooft, Pieter
Duarte, Francesca: 131, 157
Dudley, Robert, earl of Leicester: 135
Duijester, William: 168
Dunkirk privateers: 35
Dutch Academy: 100–101

181

Dutch diplomacy, importance of Holland in: 37
Dutch East India Company: 24, 53, 57, 69ff., 75, 86, 113; directors of, 70
Dutch fisheries: 56, 61
Dutch language: 84, 100, 118–19, 123–30; influence of French Renaissance on, 128
Dutch trade: 63, 68–69, 70, 74–75
Dutch painting: 159

East India Company: see Dutch East India Company
East India House: 146
East Indiamen: 58, 70
East Indian service: 56
East Indian trade: 58
East Indies: 51–54, 62, 66–67, 73
Eckhout, Susanna: 124
Edam, synod at: 153
Education: 92–95, 97
Egberts, Dr. (anatomy teacher): 164
Eglantier: see chambers of rhetorics
Elias, Nicholas: 163–64
Elsharmer, Adam: 164
Elzevier, Daniel: 111–12, 115
Elzevier, Lodewijk: 92, 111–12
Elzevier press: 84, 110, 158
Emblem books: 125
Emden, Francis van den: 106
England: 22, 29, 43, 125, 158, 167; Dutch trade with, 63, 65, 75, 77, 82, 84; book trade with, 84; financial relations with, 87–89; intellectual life of, 90; influence on Bredero of, 139
English Anabaptists: 11
English Calvinists: 11
English East India Company: 73
English Muscovy Company: 58

English Presbyterians' Orphanage: 93
English West Indies: 73
Engraving: 169ff.
Episcopius, Simon: 105
Erasmus, Desiderius: 29, 110, 120, 122
Erp, Christina van: *see* Hooft, Christina
Estates of Holland: 32, 41
Etching: 169ff.
Euclid: 94
Europe: 166; trade with Amsterdam of, 64, 67, 69, 87
Evelyn, John: 160
Evertsz., Jan: 158
Exchange Bank: 8, 16, 19, 24, 53, 59, 86–87; commission for, 21; financial policy of, 84, 86, 89–90; depositors in, 85

Fabritus, Carel: 164–65
Farar, David: 99
Far East: 69
Fargel, Caspar: 42
Farnese, Allessandro, duke of Parma: 50, 57
Feltham, Owen: 4–5, 16
Fish market: 8–9; mongers in, 7
Flanders: 50, 159
Flinck, Govert: 165
Florence: 128
Floris V: 129
Florisz., Balthazar: 82
Flute (fluit): 56
Fluweelenburgwal: 9
Food: 8, 16–18
Fortifications: 7, 13, 19
Fouquet, Nicolas: 58
France: 29, 43, 50, 58, 90, 96, 158; Dutch trade with, 63, 65, 74
Franeker, university of: 98
Frederick I of Prussia: 109

Index

Frederick Henry, Prince: 32, 34–35, 37–38
Freemantle, Katharine: 20
French Huguenots: 11, 81
French Jansenists: 112
French mercantilists: 58
French West Indies: 73
Friesland: 57

Gabbema, Hayo: 95
Gables: plain triangle (*tuit-gevel*), 9, 13; stepped (*trap-gevel*), 9, 13; bell (*klokgevel*), 14; popular neck (*halsgevel*), 14
Gaeff, Maria Claes: 162
Galileo: 91
Geer, Louis de: 36; trading interests of, 64–65, 88
Geer, Matthais de: 64
Gelderland: 41
Genoa: 53
George I of England: 108
Gerard, Stevan: 64
German Calvinists: 11
German Lutherans: 11
Germany: 65, 95–96
Geyl, Pieter: 46ff., 135
Gibraltar, Straits of: 65
Goethe, Johann Wolfgang von: 146
Goa: 68
Goldsmiths: 10
Gomarus, Franciscus: 28
Gooiland: 96, 130
Gothenburg: 63
Gouda: 67
Graaf, Reinier de: 107
Grachts: *see* canals
Graeff, Andries de: 42–43
Graeff, Cornelis de: 40–41
Graeff, Jacob de: 32ff., 40, 119–20
Grain exchange: 62

Grand Pensionary of Holland: *see* Advocate
Gravenstraat: 82, 114
Great Britain: 39, 64
Greek Orthodox Church: 11
Green, Robert: 140
Greenland: 53, 75
Grierson, Sir Herbert: 134
Grog shops: 8
Grootenhuys, Arent ten: 74
Grotius, Hugo: 30, 62, 113, 131, 149; arrest of, 31; on Catholicism, 146
Guicciardini, Lodovico: 50
Guildhalls: 7, 19
Guilds: 77–80
Gulden Wan: 151
Guinea: 66
Gustavus Adolphus of Sweden: 65, 88

Haarlem: 67, 74, 142, 147, 161, 165
Haga, Cornelis: 65
Hague, The: 24, 30, 106, 153, 164
Hals, Dirk: 156
Hals, Frans: 163
Hamburg: 63
Hamm, Stephan: 108
Hancock, Richard: 157
Hanseatic League: 49, 51–52, 61, 63
Hart, Dr. Simon: 57, 81
Harvey, Dr. William: 108
Hasselaer, Peter: 68
Hat making: 10
Hebrew School: 106
Heemskerck, Jacob van: 67
Heemskerk, Johann van: 130–31
Heemskerk, Maarten van: 154
Heereboord, Adrianus: 106
Heeren: 18, 21, 32, 52, 64, 80, 87, 102–104, 117; Baltic diplomacy

of, 36ff.; conflict with William II, 39; evaluation of, 44ff.; as representatives of Amsterdam, 44, 47; trade influences of, 71, 84; on music, 153-56

Heeren XVII: *see* East India Company, directors

Heeren XIX: *see* West India Company, directors

Heidelberg Catechism: 118

Heineken brewery: 74

Heinsius, Daniel: 96, 129, 138

Hellemans, Helcornora: *see* Hooft, Helcornora

Helst, Bartholomeus van der: 136, 161, 163, 165; evaluation of, 165ff.

Henrietta, Princess: 120

Henry IV of France: 58, 135

Herengracht: 6-7, 9, 12, 14, 40, 81, 88

Herring packers: 74

Heyn, Piet: 34, 55, 72

Hierpoort: 97

Highmore, Dr. (dentist) : 108

Hitten, Casper van: 115-16

Hitten, Jansz.: 115

Hobbema, Meindert: 136, 166

Hobbes, Thomas: 110

Hogerbeets, Rombout: 31

Holland: 24, 97, 110, 155, 169; Count of, 21; Estates of, 26; anti-Orange party in, 41; trade of, 51, 66, 69, 72, 89; universities in, 103; painting in, 159-60

Homan, Hermann: 106

Homes: 4, 10, 13, 15

Hondécoter, Melchoir de: 168

Hondius, Jodocus: 92, 111-12, 171; Mercator *Atlas* of, 111

Hooch, Pieter de: 136

Hooft, Christina: 130, 157

Hooft, Cornelis: 28-30, 45-46, 51, 96

Hooft, Helconora: 132

Hooft, Pieter Cornelisz.: 92, 96-97, 100, 103, 113, 121ff., 137-38, 146, 153, 156-58; dramatic writings of, 128-29; poetry by, 130-34; histories by, 135-36

Hooft, Pieter Jansz.: 119

Hoogh, Pieter de: 161, 168

Hooghe, Romeijn de: 171

Hoogstraat: 11

Hoote, Pieter: 73

Hop, Cornelis: 43

Horace: 95

Hortus Botanicus: 105

Hortus Medicus: 104

Hosiers: 9

Houses: *see* homes

Hout, Jan van: 160

Houtman, Cornelis: 67-68

Howell, James: 5, 10, 54

Hudson, Henry: 60

Huygens, Christiaan: 109

Huygens, Constantijn: 125-26, 129, 131, 156; on music, 153-54

't Huys te Sinnelust: 101-102

Huysum, Samuel van: 168

IJ: 3, 5-7, 12-13, 97

IJsselmeer: 35-37, 51-52

India: 67-69; trade with, 58

Indian Ocean: 152

Industries: 7

Insurance Commission: 21

"Island of California": 111

Israël, Manasseh ben: *see* Manasseh ben Israël

Italy: 96, 128, 158; trade with, 65, 90; humanism in, 128

Jacobsz., Dirck: 162

Index

James I of England: 31, 156
Janssonius, Johannes: 84, 11–14, 171
Janszoon, Willem: 112; see also Janssonius, Gulieumus and Bleau, Willem Jansz.
Jarchi (Raschi) : 98
Jardin, Karel de: 170
Java: 68
Jelles, Jarig: 107
Jerusalem: 97
Jesuit: 106
Jewelers: 10
Jewish community: 10–11, 60, 66, 77; Sephardem, 10–11, 60, 98, 105; synagogues of, 10–11; Ashkenaem, 11, 60; Marranoes, 105
John of Saxe-Weimar: 65
Jonson, Ben: 139
Joodenbreestraat: 174

Kalbergen, Elizabeth: 124
Kalff, Walter: 168
Kalverstraat: 11
Kampen, Cornelis van: 122
Karels, Adam: 124
Keere, Pieter van den: 111
Keizergracht: 12–14, 83, 100, 131
Ketel, Cornelis: 162
Keyser, Hendrik de: 12, 57, 117, 129
Keyser, Thomas de: 136, 163–64
Kick, Simon: 168
Klokkenspels: 155–56
Kloosterstraat: 93
Kloveniersburgwal: 7, 13–14, 83, 88
Kloveniers Guild: 162
Koelstraat: 98
Königsberg: 63
Koninck, Philips: 166
Korenbeurs: see grain exchange
Krul, Jan Hermansz.: 75

Laemer, Thomas: 99
Lairesse, Gérard de: 136, 161, 166, 171
Landjuweel: see Chambers of Rhetorics
Lassus, Orlandus: 153
Lastman, Pieter: 136, 163
Latin America: 66
Latin schools: 91, 93, 98, 102
Laud, William, Archbishop of Canterbury: 37
Leeuwenhoek, Anthonie van: 92, 105, 107–108
Legal restrictions: 83
Leicester, earl of: see Dudley
Leiden: 10, 28, 33, 97, 99, 115, 126, 154, 161, 163; university of, 33, 93, 96, 99, 102; textile, trade in, 78; Rembrandt and, 83; printing in, 110–112
Lepers' House: 165
Levant, the, and Levantines: 11, 66
Leyster, Judith: 168
Libertines: 28, 122, 147; Calvinist persecution of, 32; see also Remonstrants
Lieve Vrouwegilde: 159
Limborch, Philippe van: 105
Linschoten, Jan van: 116; overseas explorations of, 67–68
Lipsius, Justius: 33
Lisbon: 104
Literature: 119, 152
Locke, John: 26, 91–92, 105, 112
Loire River: 74
Lombard brokers: 89
Lombok: 68
London: 59, 146, 167; sugar manufacturing in, 75, 82; culture of, 90
Lossy, Joannes: 154
Lossy, Nicholas: 154

Lossy, Willem: 154
Louis XIV of France: 40, 43, 45, 57, 65, 155
Low Countries: 3, 43, 52; commerce in, 51; geographers of, 111
Luik: 161
Lutherans, Bible of: 110

Madagascar: 68
Maes, Nicholas: 16, 136, 161, 165
Magnificat, office of: 29, 40, 42
Magnus, Albert: 112
Mallhysz., Paulus: 158
Malphigi, Marcello: 108
Manesseh ben Israël: 92, 98, 106
Mander, Carel van: 159
Mansfeld, Count Ernest: 65
Margriete, beloved of Bredero: 143
Maritime Affairs, Commission for: 21
Market places: 9, 16, 77
Marlowe, Christopher: 139
Marvell, Andrew: 62
Maryland: 73
Mauritshuis: 164
Maurice, Prince of Nassau: 27, 31, 33
May Aaltje: 143
Mayflower: 114
Maximilian I, Emperor: 49
Mediterranean: 65–66
Meisnerus, Eusebius: 102
Mels, Dirck: 58
Mels, Gysberto: 58
Mengelberg, Willem: 155
Mennonites: 11, 101; orphanage of, 93
Meslage, Gerrit: 158
Mercator, Rumoldus: 111
Merchants: 9
Metsu, Gabriel: 161, 168

Meyer, Lodewijk: 107
Middle Ages, Amsterdam in: 77, 90
Middleburg: 71
Military guilds: *see schutterij*
Milton, John: 149
Minuit, Peter: 73
Moeyaert, Claes: 170
Moeyaert, Cornelisz.: 164
Molucca: 68
Montaigne, Michel Eyquem, seigneur de: 130, 134
Montchriétien, Antoyne de: 48
Morteira, Saul Levi: 106
Mot, Philip del: 158
Moyaert, Nicolaes: 136
Muiden Castle, circle at: 96–97, 122–23, 130–32, 156–57
Münster, peace of: 38
Muntplein: 6, 83
Music: 117, 153; madrigals, 139; church and organ, 153–54; composition, 155; public performance of, 155–58; popular, 156–57; instruments, 157–58; publishing, 158

Naarden: 171
Narva: 63
Naseby: 37
Nash, Thomas: 17
Naval docks: 19
Neck, Jacob van: 69
Nelscher, C.: 156
Nes, the: 137, 142
Netherlands: 39, 146, 149, 156, 167; first map of, 159
New Amsterdam: 60; trade with, 72–73
Newfoundland: 52, 61
New Sweden: 73
Nieuwe Kerk: 8, 98, 104, 107;

Vondel's grave in, 152; organ in, 154
Nieuwe Zijde: 91
Nieuwendijk: 82
Nieuwe Nieuwestraat: 101
Noons, Reiner: 170
Noord, Jacob van: 154
North America: 83
Northern Europe: 36
North Holland: 57
Northmen: 60
North Sea, the: 49, 51–52, 63
Norway: 63
Nova Zembla: 67

Occo, Anna: 162
Oetgens, Frans: 12
Oldenbarnevelt, John van: 27, 29–33, 69, 71, 149; Arminian controversy, 27ff.
Oostsanen, Jacob van: 159–60, 162, 169
Oostzijd van de Singel: 93
Oostzide van het Nieuwe Brug: 59
Orange, House of: 40–41; party, 41
Osborne, Thomas (Earl of Danby) : 85
Ostade, Adriaan van: 15, 136, 138, 145–46, 167
Osterburg: 75
Ostend, privateers from: 35
Oude Kerk: at Amsterdam, 8–9, 15, 59, 91, 151, 156, 174; organ in, 153–54; at Delft, 109
Oudenbrug: 62
Oude-Zijdsvoorburgwal: 137, 152
Oude Wal: 7
Overijssel: 41
Overseas explorations: 66–67
Ovid: 96, 148
Oxford, university of: 103

Paget, John: 98
Painting, relation of to literature: 136; patrons of, 159–61; Regent pieces and portraits, 162ff.; Biblical, 162–64; chiaroscuro, 163ff.; historical, 163; landscape, 166ff.; genre, 137, 167ff.; still life, 168–69
Pampus (mudbank) : 6
Pardo, Joseph: 99
Paris: 90
Parliament, English: 61
Parma: *see* Farnese
Passe, Cornelis van der: 126, 144, 157
Passe, Crispijn de: 171
Pauw, Adriaan: 41
Pauw family: 42
Pauw, Reynier: 29ff., 41, 68
Pepys, Samuel: 58, 95, 115, 168
Pensionaris: see Advocate
Peter I of Russia: 58, 95, 108
Philip of Burgundy: 85
Philip II of Spain: 57
Pietersz., Doen: 110
Pijlsteeg: 94
Pilgrim Fathers: 10, 114
Plancius, Petrius: 27ff., 98, 111; influence on overseas explorations, 66–67
Plantins (printers in Leiden) : 110
Plasterers: 79
Plautus: 124, 129
Plemp, Cornelis Gijsbertsz.: 60
Plemp, Cornelis Plempsz.: 131
Poetry: occasional, 120–121; lyrical, 136–37
Poor relief: *see Weeskammer*
Portugal and the Portuguese: 50, 58; trade influences of, 65–68; refugees from, 66, 88
Potter, Paulus: 166

Pietersz., Aert: 164
Prinsengracht: 12, 152
Printing: 84
Privy Council, English: 61
Protestants: 50, 147
"Provisions of Amsterdam": 49
Pubs: 8
Puritans, English: 139
Pijlsteeg: 151
Pynas, Jan Symonsz.: 163-64

Quakers: 11
Quast, Pieter: 168
Quays: 4
Quekels, Ida: 130

Renaissance, Dutch: 4, 19
Rabbah, Brershit: 98
Raleigh, Sir Walter: 58, 62
Ram, J. de: 12, 171
Rasphuis: 57
Reael, Laurens: 131
Reformation: 19, 153
Reformed Church, Dutch: 30, 97,
   102, 104; on civil marriage, 21;
   Amsterdam *classis* of, 24
Refugees: 10, 27ff.
Regents: *see* Heeren
Regulierspoort: 157
Regulierstoren: 93, 156
Religion in Amsterdam: 24 ff.
Rembrandt van Rijn: 5-8, 10,
   12, 14, 18, 23, 45, 54, 57, 83, 99,
   104, 117, 128, 152, 158, 161-64,
   169; financial problems of, 21,
   172-73; students of, 164; com-
   pared to genre painters, 167;
   etchings of, 170; evaluation of,
   171ff.; as mirror of Amster-
   dam, 173-74
Rembrandt, Cornelia: 172
Rembrandt Plein: 174
Rembrandt, Saskia: 5, 172-74

Rembrandt, Titus: 172
Remonstrants, the: 28ff., 34, 102-
   103, 111, 147; seminary of, 105
Restaurants: 8
Reymont III: 162
Rieuwertsz., Jan: 107
Riga: 63
Rijksmuseum: 33, 152
Rijnback, Dr. A. A. van: 140
Rijn, Rembrandt van: *see* Rem-
   brandt van Rijn
Rijnsburg: 106
Rijp, Jan Cornelisz. de: 67
Robinson, John: 97
Rodenburg, Dirk: 123
Rogers, Estienne: 158
Rogge (widow in business) : 55
Rokin (stretch of Amstel) : 5, 7,
   13, 59, 157
Roman Catholic Europe: 49
Roman Catholicism: 24, 28, 50;
   60; Church of Onze Liever
   Heer op Zolder, 11; treatment
   of, 25ff., 37; Vondel's conver-
   sion to, 147-48; Tesselschade's
   conversion to, 148
Roman Forum: 96
Roonhuysen, H. van: 105
Rosengracht: 172
Rotterdam: 161
Round Church: 11
Royal Exchange, London: 85
Royal Palace: *see* Amsterdam
   City Hall
Royal Society, England: 107
Rubens, Peter Paul: 151
Rupert, Prince of the Palatinate:
   169
Russia: 63, 67, 75, 87
Ruysch, Frederik: 105, 108-109
Ruysch, Rachael: 168
Ruysdael, Jacob: 7, 136, 161, 166;
   etchings of, 170

Index

St. Anthonie's Weigh House: 9, 104

St. Eloyengilde: 80

St. Joris Voetboogdoelen: 162

St. Lucas Guild: 79, 159, 161

St. Nicholas Church: 9

St. Nicholas market: 8

St. Olaf's Chapel: 9, 59

St. Olaf's gate: 9

St. Thomas (island of) : 66

Savery, Jac.: 170

Scaliger, Joseph: 99

Scheldt River: 35, 51

Schools: 16

Schouwburg: 174; performances in, 155

Schout: see sheriff

Schrierstoren: 60, 151

Schutterij (military guilds) : 138, 160, 162; discussion of, 23ff.; role in Arminian controversy, 28

Sea, influence on Amsterdam of: 3ff.

Sea Beggars: 49

Seghers, Hercules: 163, 166; etchings by, 170; compared to Rembrandt, 173

Selden, John: 62

Seneca: 95–96, 126, 128

Serwouter, Pieter: 170

Seville: 84

Shakespeare, William: 67, 95, 139, 146

Sheriff: 21–22

Shiller, G. H.: 107

Shipping: 7

Ships' camels: 6

Shoemakers and tanners: 10, 78

Shops and stores: 4, 10

Singel River: 6–7, 46, 97, 152, 157

Sitwell, Sacheverell: 167

Slade, Matthew: 98–99, 104

Sluices: 7

Snellius, Rudolph: 33

Social classes: see Amsterdam, social classes

Socinians: 109

Söderkompanie: 73

Soestdijk: 40

Solmo, Amelia von: 120

Sophocles: 95

Sound: see Danish Sound

South Church: 156

South Netherlands: 35, 57, 72, 153, 157; school of painting of, 159

Spain: 38, 51, 53, 55; truce with, 27; navy of, 56, 84; trade with, 65–66, 71–72, 88; Jewish policy of, 66

Sparendammerburg: 61

Speed, John: 111

Spinhuis: 130

Spieghel, Anna: 130

Spieghel, Brechtje: 130

Spieghel, Hendrik: 120, 122, 128, 130

Spieghel, Jan: 130

Spieghel, Laurensz.: 60

Spinoza, Benedictus de: 91–92, 105–108

Spitzbergen: 67

Shrewsbury, earl of: see Talbot, Charles

Stadthouders Kade: 6, 152

Staelpaert, Daniel: 20

Staets, Hendrik: 12

Starter, Jan Jansz.: 121, 137, 143, 153, 158

States General: 24, 26, 28, 30, 36, 98; defense policies of, 38, 65; siege of Amsterdam by, 39; commercial policies of, 67–71; financing of, 87

States of Holland: 37, 41, 103;

military policies of, 38; relations with William II, 43; trade policies of, 66

Steen, Jan: 15, 136, 138, 145–46, 156, 167

Stockholm: 63

Stockmanx, Magdalena: 143

Stoffels, Hendrikje: 25, 172

Stoopendaal, E.: 82

Street vendors: 7, 10

Streets, named after occupations: 80–81

Stuart, Mary, Princess of Orange: 35, 41, 96

Stuart, Mary, Queen of Scotland: 149

Suasso, Baron: 88

Sublime Porte, the: 66

Surinam: 53

Swammerdam, Jan: 109

Swanton in Norwich, England: 97

Sweden: 36, 43, 51, 57, 73; munitions trade with, 64–65; copper mines of, 88

Sweelinck, Dirk: 154

Sweelinck, Jan Pietersz.: 117, 154, 157, 175; musical compositions of, 154–55

Swiss Academy: 102

Syndics of the Cloth Hall: 10

Tacitus: 136

Talbot, Charles (Earl of Shrewsbury) : 85

Taverns: 9

Teile-Sichting, P. A.: 112

Temple, Sir William: 15, 86

Teniers, David: 138

Terrence: 142

Tesselschade: see Visscher, Maria

Texel quay: 74

Thargum (Hebrew scholar) : 97

Theater: 118; connections with charity, 118, 125; Chambers of Rhetorics and, 123, 125; actors and actresses, 124–25; Coster's Academy and, 125; patronage of, 125

Theunisz., Jan: 99, 101–102, 157

Thibaut: 55

Tongerloo, Abraham van: 83

Town fathers: see Heeren

Tradesmen's shops: 9–10

Trigland, Jacob: 30–31

Trip, Elias: 64, 88

Trip family: 36, 42

Trip, Hendrick: 64

Trip, Jacob: 64

Trip, Louis: 64, 74

Triple Alliance of 1668: 42–43

Tulp, Dr. Nicholass: 18, 46, 92, 104, 120, 164

Turkish: 60, 65

Turner, Joseph: 166

't Wit Lavender: see Chambers of Rhetorics

United Provinces, the: 22, 24, 26–27, 43

United States of America: 166

Usselincx, Willem: 27, 73

Utrecht: 6, 30

Uyttenbogaert, Johannes: 28, 30, 34

Valcknier, Gillis: 42, 44

Van Nuyts: 81

Varkenssluis: 137

Vechters, Joan: 122

Veen, Adriaan van der: 119

Vega, Joseph de la: 99

Velde, Adriaen van der: 166–67, 170

Velde, Esais van de: 136

Velde, Jan van den: 94

Index

Velde, William van der (the elder) : 167

Velde, William van der (the younger) : 167

Velsen Geeraerdt van: 129

Venice: 4, 50, 52–53, 98, 104; exchange of, 84, 87

Vermeer, Jan: 136, 171

Verona: 164

Versailles: 45

Vinckboons, David: 166–67; etchings of, 170

Vingboons, Philips: 14

Virgil: 149

Virginia: 74

Visby: 49

Visscher, Anna: 131

Visscher, Claes Jansz.: 170

Visscher, Maria: 131, 138, 143, 148, 157, 175; conversion to Catholicism, 148

Visscher, Roemer: 113, 122, 136, 175

Vleeshaals: 77

Vlieger, Simon de: 161, 167

Vollenhove, Joannes: 132

Voltaire, François Marie Arouet de: 55, 91

Vondel, Anna: 152

Vondel, Joost van der: 5–7, 9, 19, 60, 92, 94–96, 103, 113–14, 117, 124, 126, 136–38, 141, 145, 153, 158, 174; on Calvinists, 32; on the Bickers, 44; dedication of City Hall by, 44; on Amsterdam warehouses, 75; family affairs of, 77; occasional poetry by, 120–21, 148; in Chambers of Rhetorics, 121; friendship with the Visschers, 122; plays by, 125ff.; as Amsterdam's poet, 145–46; evaluation of, 146–47; dramatic writings by, 148–49;

on music, 156, 165

Vondel Park: 152, 174

Voorburg: 106

Vos, Jan: 125

Voscuyl, Dirk Pietersz.: 158

Vossius, Geradus Joannes: 102–103, 113

Vries, Simon Joosten de: 106

Vroedschap: see Heeren

Waag, the: 7, 159

Waerwyck, Wybrand van: 69

Wagenaar, Jan: 19

Waghenaer, Lucas Jansz.: 110–11

Walenpleintje: 11

Walloons: 72, 167; orphanage of, 93, 147

Walpole, Horace: 167

Warehouses: 6, 10, 13, 15–16, 19

Warmoesgracht: 81

Warmoesstraat: 8–10, 13, 59, 94, 137, 151, 174

Warmussgasse: 75

Waterland: 138

Waterloo Plein: 76, 174

Water supply: 5

Weenick, Jan Baptist: 168

Weeskammer: 89, 126

Weesp: 130

Weevers, Theodoor: 128, 133, 145

West Church: 156

West India Company, Dutch: 27, 32, 34, 53, 71–73; directors of, 71

West Indies: 53

Wettelijk: see legal restrictions

Weyden, Roger van den: 160

Whitehall: 45

White Sea: 53, 96, 152

William I, Prince of Orange: 34, 135

William II, Prince of Orange: 35, 38ff., 40–41; political strength

of, 38; death of, 39; treaty with Amsterdam, 39
William III, Prince of Orange: 40–42, 171; as stadtholder-king, 39; as stadtholder, 43
Witsen, Nicholas: 95
Witt, Jan de: 40, 42, 106–107; politics of, 40–41; alliance with Cromwell, 41
Witt, Wendela de: 40
Witt, Witte de: 37, 161, 168

Woerden Jansz. van: 110
Woerden, Herman van: 129
Women, status of: 16

Zaandaam: 54, 57–58
Zeedijk: 151
Zeeland: 51, 66, 69–71
Zucato, Abraham: 99
Zuid-Polsbroed, Vrijheer van: see De Graeff
Zuider Zee: see IJsselmeer

THE CENTERS OF CIVILIZATION SERIES, of which this volume is the twenty-first, is intended to include accounts of the great cities of the world during particular periods of their flowering, from ancient times to the present. The following list is complete as of the date of this volume:

1. Charles Alexander Robinson, Jr. *Athens in the Age of Pericles.*

2. Arthur J. Arberry. *Shiraz: Persian City of Saints and Poets.*

3. Glanville Downey. *Constantinople in the Age of Justinian.*

4. Roger Le Tourneau. *Fez in the Age of the Marinides.* Translated from the French by Besse Alberta Clement.

5. Henry Thompson Rowell. *Rome in the Augustan Age.*

6. Glanville Downey. *Antioch in the Age of Theodosius the Great.*

7. Richard M. Kain. *Dublin in the Age of William Butler Yeats and James Joyce.*

8. Glanville Downey. *Gaza in the Early Sixth Century.*

9. Bernard Lewis. *Istanbul and the Civilization of the Ottoman Empire.*

10. Richard E. Sullivan. *Aix-la-Chapelle in the Age of Charlemagne.*

11. Elizabeth Riefstahl. *Thebes in the Time of Amunhotep III.*

12. Nicola A. Ziadeh. *Damascus Under the Mamlūks.*

13. Edward Wagenknecht. *Chicago.*

14. Arthur Voyce. *Moscow and the Roots of Russian Culture.*

15. Paul Ruggiers. *Florence in the Age of Dante.*

16. Gaston Wiet. *Cairo: City of Art and Commerce.* Translated by Seymour Feiler.

17. Douglas Young. *Edinburgh in the Age of Sir Walter Scott.*

18. Richard Nelson Frye. *Bukhara: The Medieval Achievement.*

19. Walter Muir Whitehill. *Boston in the Age of John Fitzgerald Kennedy.*

20. Arthur J. May. *Vienna in the Age of Franz Josef.*

21. John J. Murray. *Amsterdam in the Age of Rembrandt.*